ER Vets

Life in an Animal Emergency Room

Thanks for fixing me up!
Tucker, Paul,
& Cate Potyzis

To my
friends in
CCU
thanks for
taking such
good care
of me
- SPOOKY

ER Vets

Life in an Animal Emergency Room

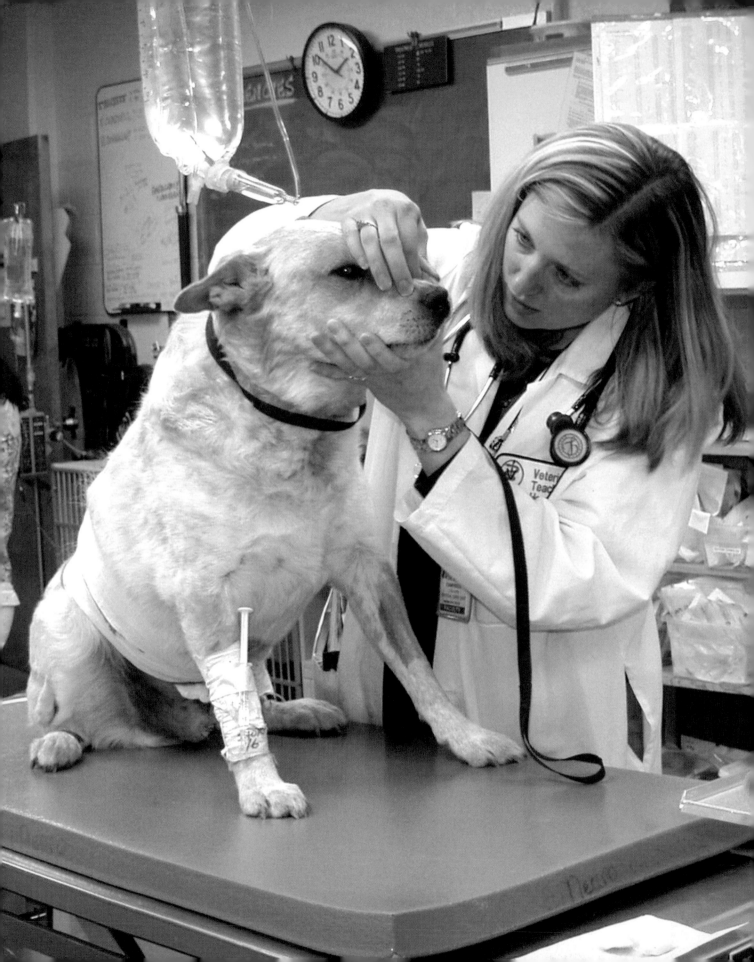

ER Vets

Life in an Animal Emergency Room

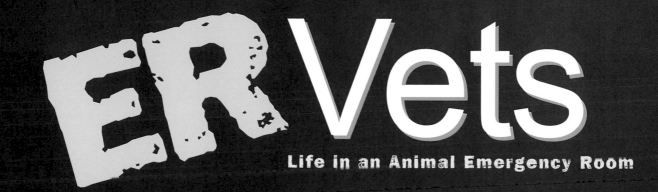

Donna M. Jackson

sandpiper

HOUGHTON MIFFLIN HARCOURT

BOSTON   NEW YORK

■ TO ALL WHO DEVOTE THEIR LIVES TO THE WELL-BEING OF ANIMALS

The Library of Congress has cataloged the hardcover edition as follows:
Jackson, Donna M., 1959–
    ER vets / by Donna M. Jackson.
        p. cm.
    Includes bibliographical references and index.
    ISBN 0-618-43663-4 (hardcover)
    1. Veterinary emergencies—Juvenile literature.
2. Veterinarians—Juvenile literature. I. Title.

SF778.J33 2005
636.089'6025—dc22
2004028231

ISBN-13: 978-0-618-43663-7
ISBN-13: 978-0-547-23758-9 pb

Book design by Lisa Diercks
Text set in Gotham.

Manufactured in Malaysia
TWP 10 9 8
4500621576

acknowLedgments

Many thanks to all the kind people at the James L. Voss Veterinary Teaching Hospital at Colorado State University who helped make this book a reality: Dr. David E. Lee, the hospital's director, who granted me access to the facility; ER vets Dr. Tim Hackett and Dr. Vicki Campbell, who generously shared their time, talents, photos, presentations, and emergency and critical care unit with me; Dr. Matt Johnston for sharing his knowledge of exotic animals and allowing me to sit in on a few surgeries; Dr. Gary Stamp for providing insight on the big emergency veterinary medicine picture; Leslie Carter, head ER nurse, for sharing her knowledge, insights, and slides; resident vets Dr. Mike Walters, Dr. Heather Connally, Dr. Darien Feary, Dr. John Chandler, Dr. Yukari Miyake, Dr. Pierre Amsellem, and Dr. Jacqueline Whittemore; all the wonderful veterinary technicians who patiently walked me though procedures — Sue Mordi, Brenda Francis, Cheryl

Resident vet Dr. Heather Connally cuddles an ER patient.

Spencer, Kim Niles, Laura Kelly, Stephanie Pitzer, Amy Mayhak, Jocey Pronko, Maura Green, Kris Obssuth, and Kim Spelts; vet students Tracey Dutson, Marty Glanzberg, Chelsea Newby, and Serena Gill; Gail Holmes; Nikki Cain; Dr. Judy Merriott; Kim Ellis; Gina Gonzales; Amanda Chandler; Dr. Erick Egger and his wife, Sue; Dr. David Twedt; Dr. Robert Callan; Gail Bishop; Bobbie Beach; Tammy Mimms; Dr. Jacob Head; Brandy Perkins; David, Jane, Rachel, and Marcus Chaknova; Dr. Steve Benscheidt; Michelle and Adam Strong; Dr. Susan Jones; Dr. Phyllis Larsen; Ken and Dianne Hackett; Rebecca Cope; Cristina Gutierrez at Vidas (www.VIDAS.org); Sandy Brown and the radiology department team; Dr. James Ross; Brian, Jenny, and Malcolm Robertson; Cheryl Nelson, University of California at Davis Veterinary School; Bill and Gail Perry; Paul and Cate Potyen; Tangie and Jayden Chambers; Jenny McGraw; Dr. Julie Bailey-Child; and Peg Queija, graphics consultant; and Charlie Kerlee, medical photographer.

A special thanks to Jenger Smith, media specialist and medical photographer at Colorado State University's Veterinary Teaching Hospital, for taking time to shoot photos and sharing many of her incredible images in the book. I'm also grateful to my editor, Ann Rider, for believing in this project and to Charlie Jackson for believing in me.

veteriNArian's oath

Being admitted to the profession of veterinary medicine, I solemnly swear to use my scientific knowledge and skills for the benefit of society through the protection of animal health, the relief of animal suffering, the conservation of animal resources, the promotion of public health, and the advancement of medical knowledge.

I will practice my profession conscientiously, with dignity, and in keeping with the principles of veterinary medical ethics.

I accept as a lifelong obligation the continual improvement of my professional knowledge and competence.

Resident vet Dr. Michael Walters examines a fourteen-year-old beagle that is having trouble breathing.

contents

Willis weighs in.

eMergeNcy!

A German shepherd . . . retreating to a corner . . . struggling to vomit . . . panting with pain. His swollen belly's tender and as tight as a drum.

His "mom" calls the animal hospital.

"Get him in here as fast as you can," says the emergency room (ER) veterinarian.

The doctor suspects the dog is suffering from a life-threatening condition called gastric dilatation-volvulus, more commonly known as GDV or "bloat." Bloat happens when a dog's stomach swells several times its normal size—usually from swallowed air—and then flips and twists in place up to 360 degrees. Not only does the twisting trap air, food, and water in the stomach, it blocks the belly's blood supply, which can kill the dog within hours.

CRITICAL INTERVENTION

BEEP . . . BEEP . . . BEEP . . . BEEP . . . BEEP

A high-pitched page signals the German shepherd's arrival at the hospital, where an ER vet is waiting to whisk the dog back to the emergency room. Immediately, he and a team of veterinary technicians (nurses) and vet students huddle around the patient to assess the dog's condition and stabilize him. They check his vital signs— heart rate, breathing, body temperature, and blood pressure—and insert an intravenous (IV) catheter (tube) into a leg vein to pump

FACING PAGE: While GDV, or bloat, affects all breeds, deep-chested dogs, such as Great Danes and German shepherds (pictured), are more at risk for developing the deadly condition.

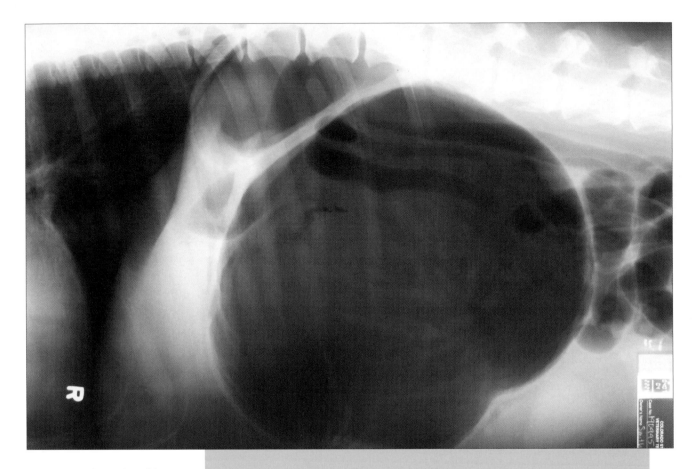

X-rays show that this German shepherd's stomach is filled with air and twisted about 180 degrees in what vets refer to as a "double bubble."

life-sustaining fluids into his body. To relieve air pressure in the dog's belly, the ER vet pushes a long flexible tube down the dog's throat and into his stomach, moving the tube forward through the twisted area so air can be released.

"At this point, the dog's probably beginning to feel more comfortable," explains ER vet Dr. Timothy Hackett. "Problem is, even though we've relieved the pressure, the stomach's still twisted. And as long as it's twisted, it's cutting off the dog's blood supply, so we absolutely have to get in there and untwist the stomach if he has any chance of survival."

During surgery—called a gastropexy—the surgeon looks for and removes any dead tissue in the stomach and other organs. The more damaged tissue, the less chance the dog has of surviving. The doctor then carefully repositions the stomach and sews it to the abdominal wall so it won't flip again.

Crisis averted . . . at least for now.

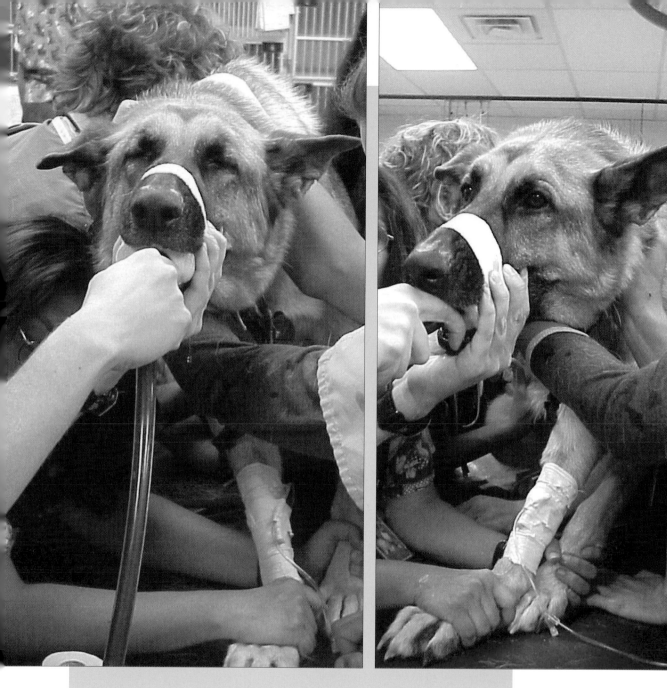

Danger to the dog's life remains after surgery, especially the first twenty-four hours. Complications such as an irregular heartbeat and low blood pressure may arise, so the ER team—now acting in its "critical care" role—uses high-tech and other equipment to monitor the dog's progress around the clock and ensure that he recovers fully. As each hour ticks by without incident, the German shepherd moves closer to returning home to his family.

To relieve air pressure in a dog's bloated belly, ER vets push a tube into its stomach. Once the tube is in place, the dog feels better, but it still needs surgery to untwist its stomach.

ANiMAL er

Medical emergencies happen. Twenty-four hours a day. Seven days a week. Dogs, cats, birds, ferrets, turtles, snakes, rabbits, guinea pigs, hamsters, chinchillas—you name it: all pets are subject to accidents and sudden illnesses, just like people. And, just like people, animals need immediate care when their health is in jeopardy.

In Colorado and nearby western states, many people bring their

seriously ill and injured pets to the emergency and critical care unit at one of the country's leading veterinary hospitals—the James L. Voss Veterinary Teaching Hospital at Colorado State University in Fort Collins. The emergency unit is staffed 24 hours a day, 365 days a year by a highly skilled team of small-animal veterinary specialists, residents, interns, nurses, and fourth-year vet students. All care deeply for animals and live for those heart-pounding, critical few moments when they can make the difference between life and death for our best friends.

"It's exciting work," says Dr. Tim Hackett, chief of emergency and critical care services, who thrives on emergency medicine's nonstop pace. "Every day you can make an impact—there's something different all the time."

The James L. Voss Veterinary Teaching Hospital at Colorado State University offers state-of-the-art medical care for animals, including emergency and critical care services 24 hours a day, 365 days a year. It's one of about 125 veterinary emergency hospitals nationwide.

BELOW: This curious Airedale terrier ventured a little too close to a porcupine.

His colleague in the ER, Dr. Vicki Campbell, agrees.

"It's extremely rewarding to take care of an animal who's near death and turn the situation into a successful one," she says. "We pour a lot of heart and energy into the animals, and it's great to see them fully recover."

Even animals that can't be saved benefit from their visit to the ER.

"I have some really memorable cases in which the animal had inoperable cancer, and we were just able to provide a fast diagnosis and give clients information so they could spend more quality time with their pets," says Dr. Hackett. "Whether that meant days or weeks—it was time they might not have had otherwise."

HUB OF THE HOSPITAL

Lights flash from a six-foot bank of monitoring and life-support machines. Oxygen seeps through the cage of a cat suffering from asthma. Fans cool a dog with a high fever.

"What's up, Sassy-pants?" a resident vet calls to a recovering tabby.

"You're doing just fine, Jasmine," a nurse reassures an ailing Labrador retriever.

No two days are alike in the emergency room, and no other veterinary specialty sees such varied cases. At any time, ER vets may treat a dog that has swallowed paintballs, has been bitten by a rattlesnake, or is suffering from heart disease; a cat that's been hit by a car, poisoned by

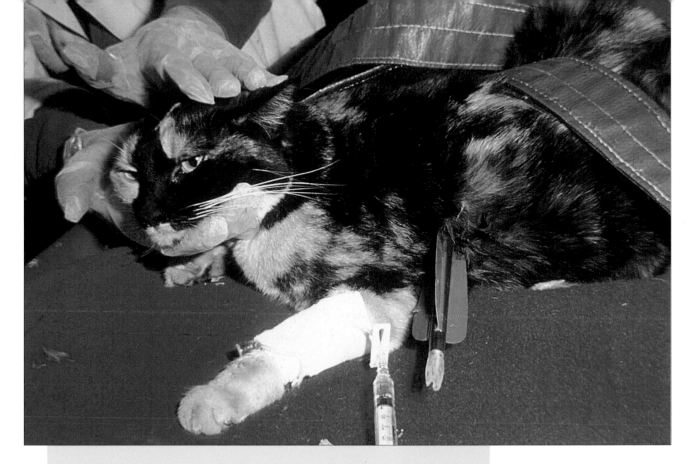

antifreeze, or in need of a blood transfusion; an alpaca with blurred vision; a bird requiring oxygen; or a hedgehog with a cancerous tumor.

One brave cat arrived at the ER with an arrow piercing his abdomen. Fortunately, the arrow missed all his major organs and doctors were able to surgically remove it. On average, the ER sees seven to ten new patients a day, about 2,500 to 3,500 a year.

Not all incoming cases pose immediate threats to life. Some require medical attention more quickly than others. To ensure that ER vets treat the most severely ill animals first, the medical team prioritizes patients' conditions using a decision-making process called triage. Triage derives from the French word *trier,* which means "to sort."

■ **PRIORITY 1:** Conditions directly interfering with vital life functions always receive top priority. Animals unable to breathe and those with heart failure, uncontrollable bleeding, urinary obstructions (can't pee), snakebites, asthma attacks, high fevers, and antifreeze poisoning all need *immediate* care. Pets suffering severe

Fortunately for this cat, the arrow missed his major organs.

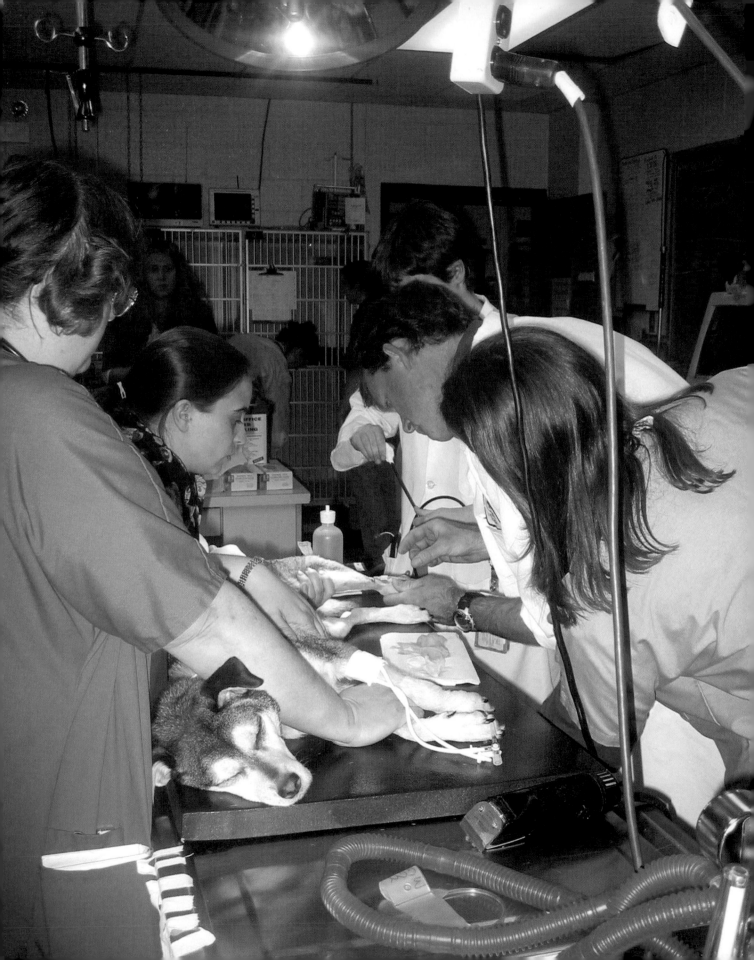

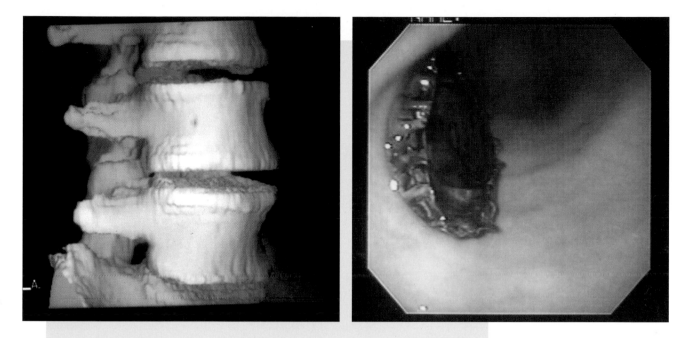

traumatic injuries—those hit by cars or attacked by other animals—also require prompt treatment.

■ **PRIORITY 2:** When an animal is likely to survive if care is given within hours—instead of minutes—its condition is deemed urgent but not immediately life-threatening. Urgent conditions include many allergic skin reactions, bladder infections, and bouts of diarrhea. These conditions may evolve into emergencies if they threaten vital life functions.

■ **PRIORITY 3:** Most animals suffering from broken bones, fractures, and lacerations (cuts) fall into the less urgent category. Their treatment may be delayed while ER vets attend to more critically ill patients.

SPEED SAVES

Once admitted to the ER, animals receive cutting-edge care from doctors, who immediately identify and treat life-threatening issues by evaluating the patient's ABCDs: airway, breathing, circulation, and disabilities. At the same time, they monitor and collect clues about the patient's overall condition. ER vets can't wait for all the answers before initiating treatments—they need to keep their patients alive so they can inch closer to a diagnosis.

State-of-the-art equipment and procedures comparable to those

ABOVE, LEFT:
Diagnostic x-rays, such as this view of a horse's spinal vertebrae, help vets see what's happening inside an animal's body.

ABOVE, RIGHT:
Endoscopes—tubes with tiny cameras at the tip—allow vets to retrieve foreign bodies such as this bottle cap from a dog's stomach.

FACING PAGE:
The ER veterinary team works on a Priority 1 emergency. Here the ER vet places an IV catheter into the dog's rear leg.

ABOVE, LEFT:
On complicated cases, ER vets consult with other specialists in the hospital, including ophthalmologists, who treat eye disorders.

ABOVE, RIGHT:
Along with traditional techniques, the hospital offers alternative treatments, such as acupuncture, for pain and other medical conditions.

in human hospitals enhance their life-saving efforts. Radiographs (x-rays), ultrasounds, magnetic resonance imaging (MRIs), and computed tomography (CT) scans help ER vets view what's happening inside an animal's body. Blood tests screen for infections and illnesses, biopsies analyze tissue from tumors, and cerebrospinal fluid taps (CSFs) help pinpoint the cause of seizures and other abnormalities.

When an animal's heart stops beating properly, the ER's cardiac defibrillator helps to restore normal beating with a jolt of electricity. A kidney dialysis system filters poisons from a dog or cat's blood and keeps the pet alive long enough for a transplant. High-tech lasers replace scalpels during some surgeries, minimizing an animal's pain and bleeding, and endoscopes—tubes with tiny cameras at the tip —offer nonsurgical ways to retrieve foreign objects, such as pennies, socks, and bottle caps, from upset stomachs.

As their patients' conditions unfold, ER vets also collaborate on cases with the hospital's top veterinary specialists, including

- **CARDIOLOGISTS,** who treat heart-related illnesses and perform open-heart and pacemaker-implant surgeries
- **ONCOLOGISTS,** who treat all types of cancers. In fact, the James L.

One of the ER team's top priorities is to ensure that animals remain comfortable and pain-free during their stay.

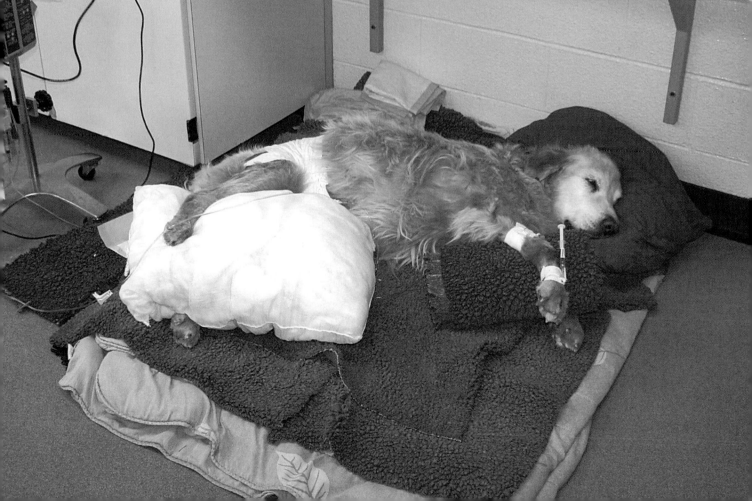

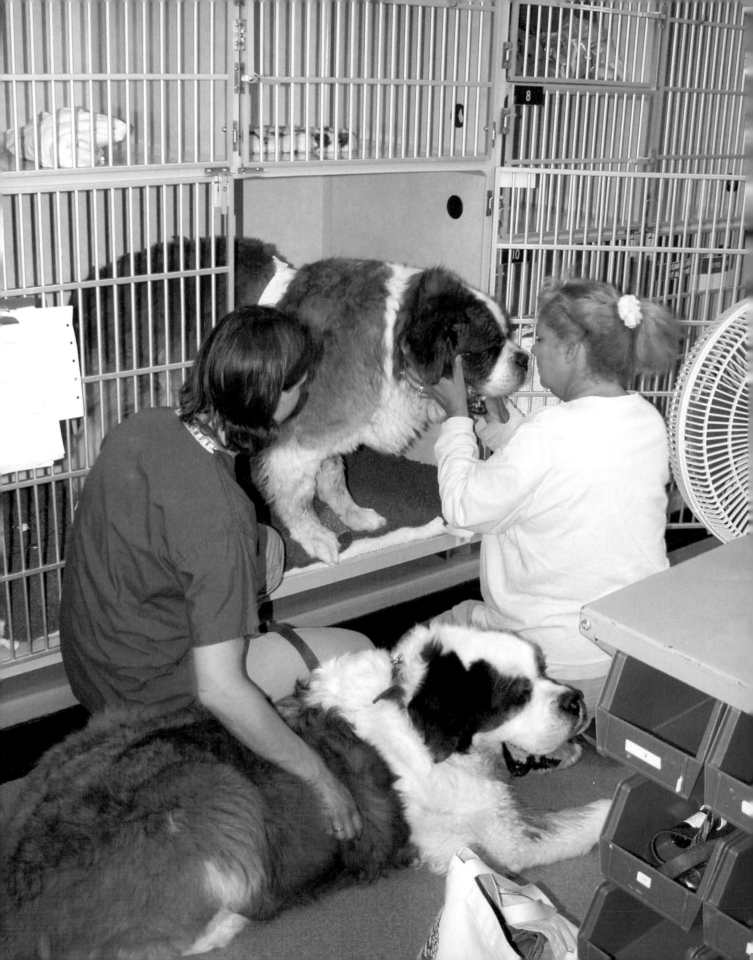

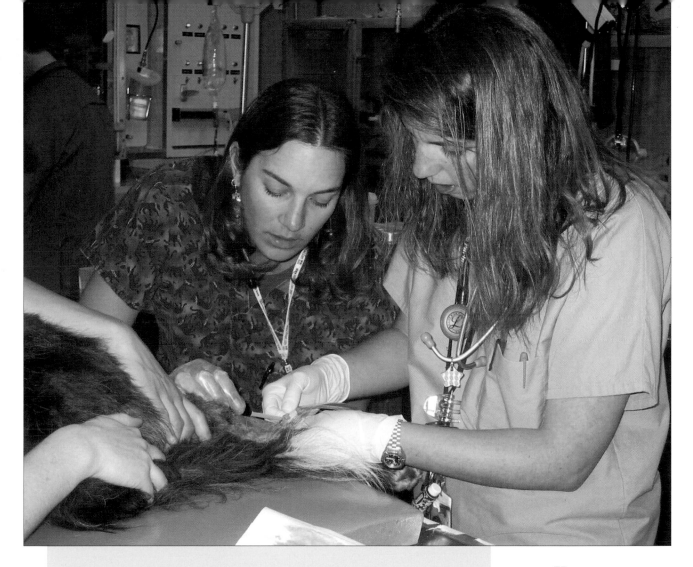

Voss Veterinary Teaching Hospital's Animal Cancer Center is recognized as *the* world leader in veterinary cancer treatments.

- **ANESTHESIOLOGISTS,** who administer medicines that relieve pain and keep animals asleep during surgery
- **NEUROLOGISTS,** who treat nervous system disorders and perform brain and spinal surgeries
- **OPHTHALMOLOGISTS,** who treat eye disorders, including cataracts and glaucoma
- **INTERNAL MEDICINE SPECIALISTS,** who treat complex illnesses involving the body's organs and systems, such as the liver, pancreas, and immune system
- **ORTHOPEDIC SURGEONS,** who repair injuries to the bones and joints

ABOVE: **ER nurse Brenda Francis walks a vet student through a procedure.**

FACING PAGE: **There's nothing like seeing a familiar face when you're not feeling well. That's why the ER team encourages family visits.**

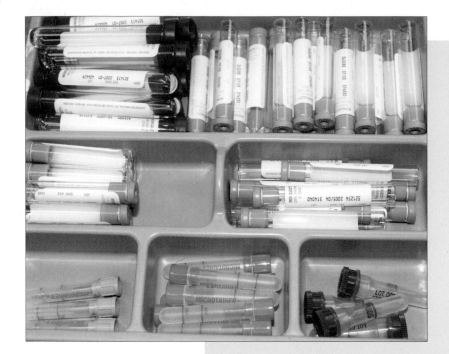

- **PATHOLOGISTS,** who analyze tissue, blood, and other samples to help diagnose diseases
- **PHARMACISTS,** who apply their knowledge of drugs to animals and their unique characteristics and diseases
- **RADIOLOGISTS,** who help perform and assess x-rays, ultrasounds, CT scans, and other ways of seeing inside the body
- **SOFT-TISSUE SURGEONS,** who remove foreign objects and tumors from animals

When ER vets need blood tests to help diagnose a problem, a patient's blood is put into tubes with different colored tops, each with a different additive depending on what's being tested. A purple top is for a complete blood count; a red top is to test the serum or liquid part of the blood; a blue top is for a test of the blood's clotting; and a green top is for testing the ammonia levels in the blood.

In all cases, the team strives to make animals as comfortable and free of pain as possible. They recognize that animals feel frightened and lonely while away from home and encourage owners to bring in favorite stuffed animals and blankets. Doctors also prescribe pain-control medications as appropriate—something rarely offered for sick animals fifteen years ago.

GROWING FIELD

Animal emergency medicine is a rapidly expanding veterinary specialty. "In the last ten years, the number of emergency clinics—those treating animals on nights and weekends when traditional vet practices are closed—has grown from about 150 to more than 700 nationwide," says Dr. Gary Stamp, executive director of the Veterinary Emergency and Critical Care Society (VECCS). At the same time, "emergency hospitals—those offering round-the-clock care and advanced medical treatments—have increased from fewer than 10 a decade ago to about 125."

One reason for the escalating interest in emergency care is that many people today consider their pets part of the family and spend more money on their medical care. The American Animal Hospital

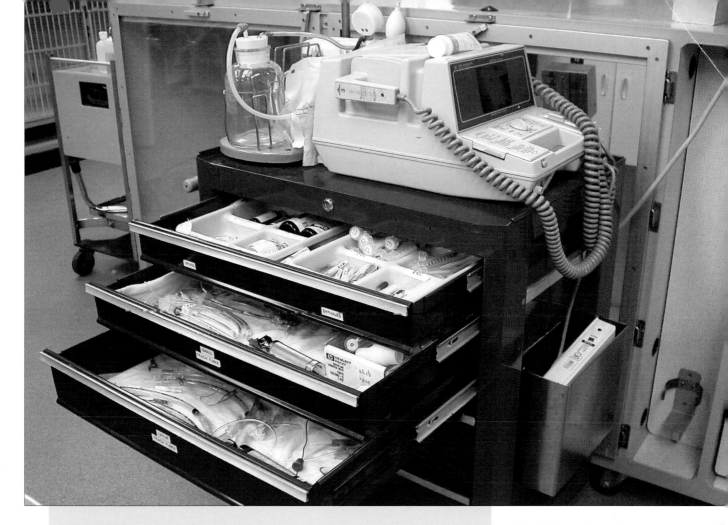

Association (AAHA) found that 83 percent of pet owners surveyed refer to themselves as their pet's "mom" or "dad," and 73 percent would go into debt to provide for their pet's well-being.

Emergency medicine "has raised the level of care available for animals beyond belief," says Dr. Stamp. "Our ER vets use advances in technology sooner than any other segment of the veterinary profession, because they always need something that works faster and better, so it will lead to a more rapid diagnosis."

With more people seeking emergency care for their pets and more advanced procedures becoming available, ER vets have greater opportunities than ever to make a difference in the lives of pets and pet owners. "Helping clients who are at their wits' end is one of the most rewarding aspects of working at a teaching hospital," says Dr. Hackett. "I like that we're that hospital of last resort—the hospital people expect can do anything."

The ER team turns to its crash cart when an animal's heart stops beating properly. The cart contains all the equipment needed to treat the patient quickly, including a defibrillator to help restore normal breathing, endotracheal tubes to place in an animal's windpipe when it stops breathing, and central vein catheters (tubes) to place near the heart so medicine can reach it quickly.

is it an emergency?

"Animals can't talk," says Dr. Hackett. "So people need to look for clues if they think their pet may be sick." Changes in behavior, heart rate, breathing, temperature, gum color, or weight can be signs of serious trouble. "You know your pet better than anyone else and can let the vet know what's normal and abnormal," says the ER vet. Arming yourself with information such as your pet's normal temperature, breathing patterns, and heart rate makes it easier to spot an emergency when it happens. Following are some signs that it's time to take your pet to the veterinarian—right away!

Rattlesnake bites to a dog's face are painful and cause its muzzle to swell. Always seek veterinary help if your dog has been bitten.

BEHAVIOR CHANGES

- Acts more aggressive, lethargic, or hyperactive
- Limps, paces, shakes, stumbles, staggers, makes noises, or licks or bites part of the body continually

HEART RATE

Faster or slower than normal

NORMAL RATES

Dogs   80–120 beats per minute
Larger and athletic dogs have slower heart rates than smaller dogs. Puppies usually have high heart rates: from 120 to 150 beats per minute.

Cats   120–160 beats per minute

Rabbits 140–220 beats per minute

Birds   150–200 beats per minute (large)

        300 beats per minute (small to medium)

        400 beats per minute (very small)

RESPIRATORY RATE

Faster or slower than normal

NORMAL RATES

Dogs   15–25 breaths per minute
Cats   20–30 breaths per minute
Rabbits 50–60 breaths per minute
Birds   12–40 breaths per minute

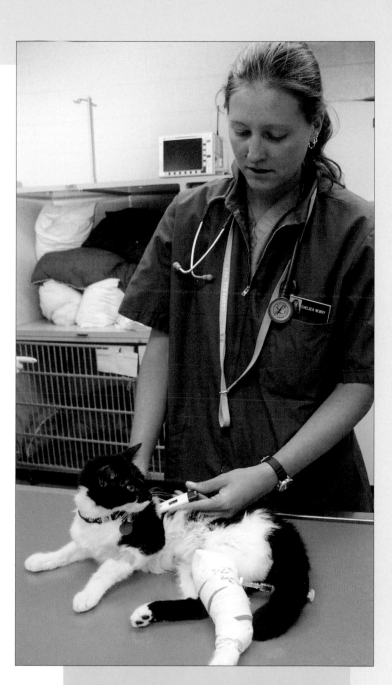

Knowing your pet's normal temperature will help you determine whether or not it has developed a fever. Temperature should be taken from the armpit, as shown, and you'll need to add one degree for accuracy.

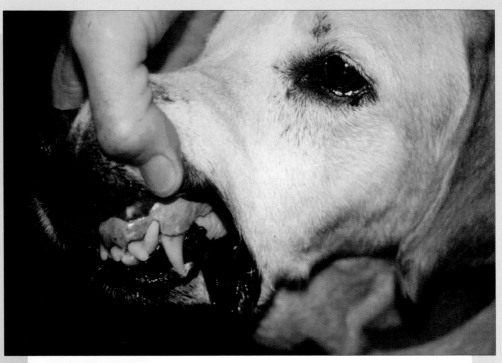

RIGHT: **A healthy dog's gums are pink; pale gums are one of the first signs of shock or anemia.**

BELOW: **Dark red gums, coupled with red eyes, can indicate a severe bacterial infection.**

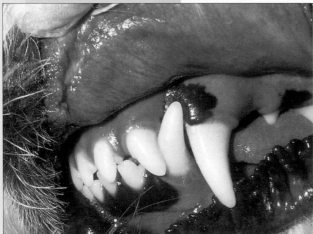

TEMPERATURE
Higher or lower than normal
Digital thermometers designed for humans work well. Temperature should be taken from the armpit (the axillary region), and you'll need to add one degree for accuracy.

NORMAL TEMPS
Dogs   101.5° F – 102.5° F
Cats   102° F – 104° F
Rabbits   102° F – 104° F

BODY WEIGHT
Noticeable weight loss or gain

OTHER INDICATORS
- Dark red or extremely pale yellow or blue-gray gums
- Unable to pee or poop, but continues to try
- Bleeding that won't stop
- Loss of or unusual gain in appetite

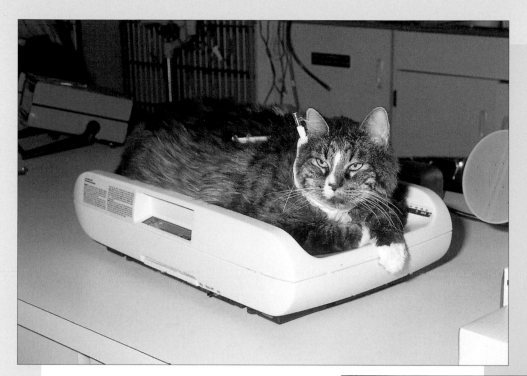

Check your pet's weight regularly so you'll know if it's gaining or losing an unusual amount—an indication that something could be wrong.

- Swollen belly, with or without vomiting
- Severe injuries from a fall, animal attack, or car accident
- Bloody diarrhea or vomit
- Eating or drinking poisons (bring the container to the vet if possible)
- Eyes twitching side to side or up and down
- Tilting head to one side, walking in circles, or banging into objects
- Gasping for air, unusually noisy breathing
- Skin that's lost its elasticity and doesn't snap back when pinched
- Collapse or seizure activity

Note: Approach all injured animals cautiously—as if they're going to bite—because when in pain, even your own animal can behave unpredictably.

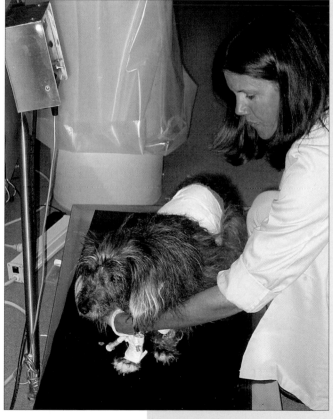

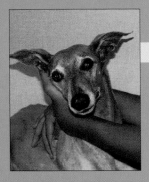

FACING: **Artist Paulus Potter's oil painting** *A Farrier's Shop* **(1648) captures the life of a Dutch "horse doctor" as he files the tooth of a frightened horse.**

vets and pets
a brief history

Caring for animals dates back centuries. Ancient "animal doctors" everywhere from China, Rome, and Egypt tended to buffalo, sheep, horses and oxen—for animals played significant religious and economic roles in early civilization. Some plowed fields, carried warriors into battle, and tracked game for hunters. Others supplied food, or were worshipped as spiritual symbols.

"As domesticated (tame) animals became increasingly valuable to human societies, a need emerged to devote a degree of attention to their health and well-being," says Joanna Swabe in her book *Animals, Disease, and Human Society.* "From the earliest known civilizations onwards, specialists in the field of animal care and animal medicine began to emerge and offer their skills and services to animals' owners."

Most ancient peoples relied on priests, shepherds, and healers to protect their animals' health, with some passing on their knowledge in writing. Egypt's Kahun Papyrus, which dates back to about 1900 B.C., is one of the oldest and most famous works addressing veterinary medicine. The document describes livestock diseases and treatments, as well as ailments of dogs, birds, and fish.

HORSE DOCTORS
Centuries later, in the Middle Ages through the late 1800s, farriers —blacksmiths who crafted iron shoes for horses to protect their

hooves — became the veterinarians of the day. Rich in practical skill, these tradesmen treated horses, which provided valuable transportation services.

Not all animals fared so well, however. During the Middle Ages, officials arrested some animals and put them on trial for crimes ranging from harassing sheep to murder.

"There's the famous case, from the fifteenth century, of a sow and her six piglets who were tried in a French court," says James Serpell, professor of humane ethics and animal welfare at the University of Pennsylvania. (The sow was convicted of strangling a young child, while her piglets "got off because they were deemed to have been minors and not fully aware of what they were doing.")

Many people believed animals could be possessed by evil forces — especially pets, such as cats, dogs, and birds. Such beliefs were "an extreme example of a general suspicion of showing affection to animals," says Jonica Newby, veterinarian and author of *Animal Attraction: Humans and Their Animal Companions.*

"For a woman living alone in the Middle Ages, keeping an animal just for companionship was potentially a death sentence — to be burnt at the stake as a witch. It all contributed to a prejudice against pet keeping that would last in Europe for centuries." The only people exempt from the rules, "to some extent," were royalty, says Serpell.

A NEW ATTITUDE

Life improved for pets in the late-eighteenth century. With western Europe's rapid rise in industry, people flocked to cities and no longer directly depended on farm animals for their livelihood. At the same time, members of society began viewing themselves more as "caretakers of the natural world, rather than controllers of it," explains Swabe. This shift in perspective helped lead to a more sentimental view of pets. Soon many middle-class city dwellers adopted small animals as companions, creating a need for their health care.

During this time, science and education also played more prominent roles, leading to the establishment of Europe's first scientific veterinary schools beginning in 1762. The United States eventually followed, establishing its first veterinary colleges in the 1850s.

Surgery demonstration circa 1940s. At that time, doctors — mostly male — performed operations on animals such as this cat without anesthesia.

Birds, such as this twenty-day-old cockatiel, and ferrets (facing page) are among the many pet animals vets treat today.

"The [U.S.] veterinary profession began its life as an urban profession devoted to caring for horses," says Susan Jones, veterinarian, historian, and author of *Valuing Animals: Veterinarians and Their Patients in Modern America.* "Veterinarians weren't located in rural areas; they were located in cities—particularly big ones like New York, Philadelphia and Boston."

That all changed at the turn of the century with the invention of the automobile. As people no longer used horses as their primary mode of transportation, veterinarians turned their attention elsewhere—first to making the livestock industry more sanitary and then to caring for companion animals, who continued to grow in popularity after World Wars I and II. Dogs especially gained favor as "worthy companions for children and adults" with the help of heroic canine stories and movie stars, such as Rin-Tin-Tin and Lassie, Jones says.

Today most veterinarians treat pet animals, which continue to grow in number. According to the 2003–4 survey of the American Pet Products Manufacturers Association (APPMA), more than 377 million pets live in 62 percent of U.S. households:

CATS	77.7 million
DOGS	65 million
BIRDS	17.3 million
REPTILES	9 million
FRESHWATER FISH	185 million
SALTWATER FISH	7 million
OTHER SMALL ANIMALS	16.8 million

Those surveyed cited "companionship, love, company, and affection" as the top benefits of keeping pets, indicating that the human-animal bond has grown stronger than ever. In 2003 alone, Americans spent $32.4 billion to care for their pets, including $7.9 billion for veterinary care and $7.2 billion for medicine and supplies.

Our interest in animals "has transformed the status of pets during the past century," says Jones. "People in America now have the money to care for their pets more extensively. But more importantly, we are willing to spend the money," she says—not because these animals provide us with food or transportation, but because they play such an integral role in our families.

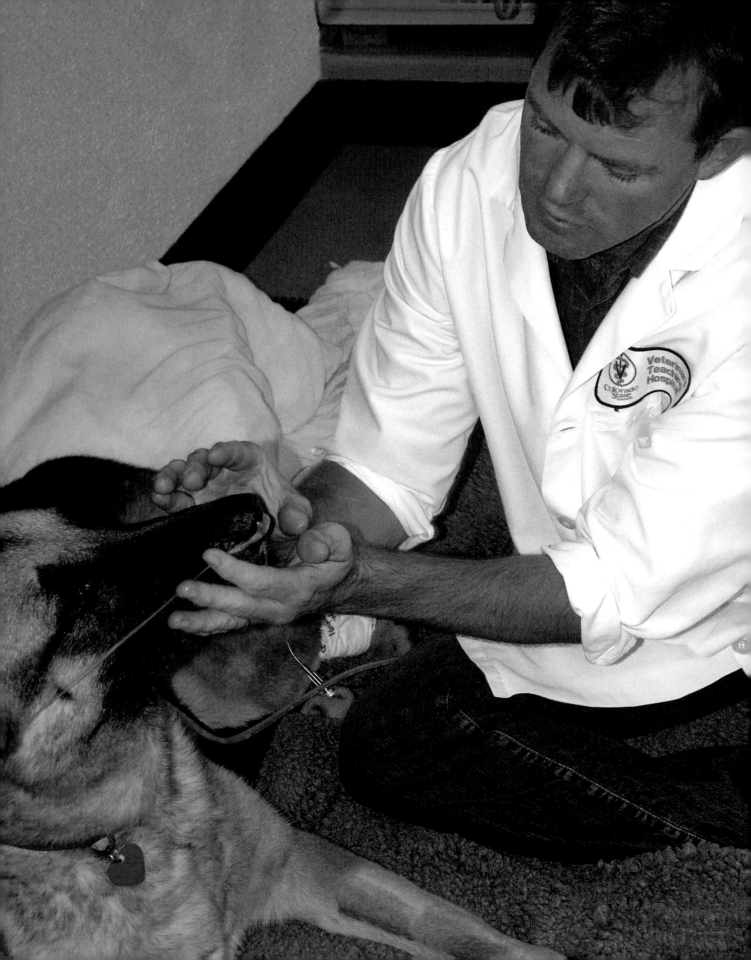

Healing Hands

d r. Tim Hackett lives life in the fast lane—personally and professionally. When he's not heading the veterinary hospital's busy emergency and critical care unit, he runs races, flies planes, sky dives, skis, kayaks, scuba dives, and mountain bikes.

"I'm an adrenaline junkie," he says. And he's not alone. Many who work in animal ERs find themselves hooked on the unpredictable days and the rewarding rush that results from bringing animals on the verge of death back to life.

Emergency vets learn to like stressful situations, says Dr. Hackett. "It also helps if you like working nights, weekends, and strange hours, because that's when the real problem cases are going to come in." Once they do, ER vets must remain calm, think on their feet, and make split-second, life-and-death decisions.

"What terrifies many people most about emergencies," says Dr. Hackett, "is that they're afraid they won't figure out what's going on quickly enough and the animal will suffer or die because of something they don't know—and we all live in fear of that. But if you're in emergency work, you learn to operate without an answer and treat life-threatening problems while you're working on the diagnosis."

BORN TO BE A VET

Dr. Hackett *always* knew he'd be a veterinarian—even as a young boy growing up in Boulder, Colorado. "Every spring, I'd bring home baby

Dr. Hackett always knew he wanted to be a vet. As a boy, he "rescued" baby birds from a nearby forest. A neighbor, Rebecca Files, painted the above portrait of young Tim with one of his birds.

FACING PAGE: Dr. Hackett helps this German shepherd breathe easier.

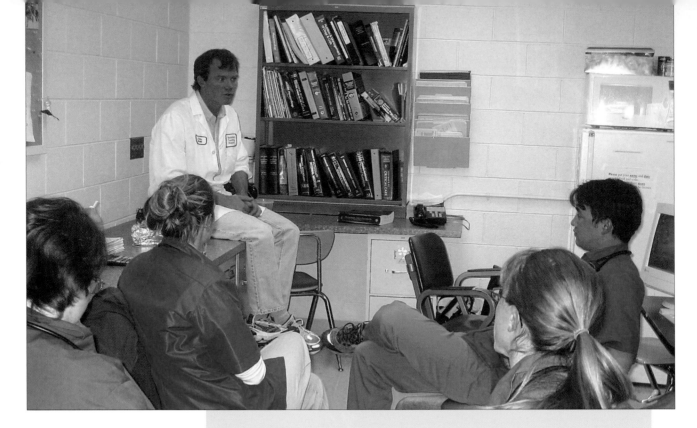

One aspect Dr. Hackett enjoys most about working at a veterinary teaching hospital is challenging students and watching them develop their skills. Dr. Hackett is an associate professor at Colorado State University.

birds that I told my parents I had 'rescued' from a nearby forest," he says. Tim helped care for the family's cats and raised pigeons as a hobby. By the time he reached high school, he worked for a local veterinarian, tending to animals and assisting with treatments.

Eight years of higher education later—four earning his bachelor's degree in zoology and four in veterinary school—and after passing a national veterinary medical board exam, Dr. Hackett officially became a veterinarian. His training didn't stop there, however.

"While I was in school, I thought I might want to be a surgeon," he says. "But I really liked emergency medicine [a new field at the time], so I went to a big emergency vet hospital in Los Angeles for a yearlong internship."

Emergency work quickly became Dr. Hackett's passion. He enjoyed it so much that he specialized in the field and spent three more years in a rigorous veterinary school program, called a residency, studying the latest techniques for diagnosing and treating life-threatening injuries and diseases in small animals. Today, he's a diplomat of the American College of Veterinary Emergency and Critical Care (ACVECC) and one of only about 136 board-certified specialists in the field worldwide.

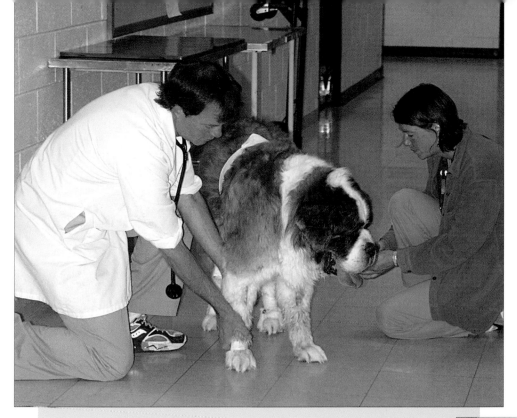

ER vets never know what each day will bring. That's part of the thrill of the job.

DAY AT A GLANCE

Dr. Hackett's workday begins at about six-thirty a.m. "I wake up in enough time to shower, feed all my pets [two dogs, two cats, and two birds], and grab a breakfast bar and newspaper on the way to work." When he arrives, he consults with the overnight doctor and nurses about patients in the hospital, and calls students, day nurses, and resident vets together for seven a.m. "rounds." During rounds, the staff reviews all the cases in the hospital and discusses treatment plans. "Together we extract all the good learning out of those cases and make a plan for the day," says Dr. Hackett.

After rounds, the twelve-hour day melts away with activity. The ER vet leads the treatment of emergencies as they come in; adjusts care and medications for hospitalized animals; consults with specialty vets on complicated cases; updates owners about their pets; completes reports and paperwork; mentors interns and residents; lectures on emergency and critical care topics; and guides veterinary students as they build their clinical skills.

"If I can stand back and let students sew up a laceration or

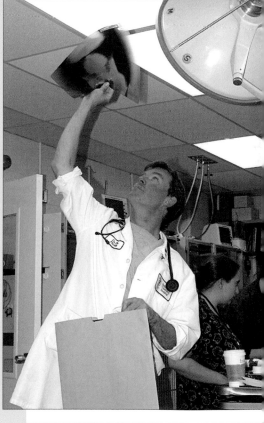

put a splint on a broken leg, it's the high point of their week," says Dr. Hackett. It's one of the things he loves most about his job, along with "interacting with all the dogs and cats and birds and other animals at the hospital."

THE MAKING OF AN ER VET

Dr. Vicki Campbell always loved animals, but didn't seriously begin thinking about being a vet until the eighth grade, when her mom gave her a book called *The Making of a Woman Vet* by Sally Haddock and Kathy Matthews. "It was very inspiring to me," she says. "Still, many of the stories were so sad that I wasn't sure I'd be able to handle things like putting animals to sleep."

Vicki volunteered at a veterinary clinic in high school and eventually discovered her calling while a junior in college, where she was a biology major. "That was the year I volunteered and was hired at an emergency practice," she says. Emergency veterinary medicine offered everything she wanted in a career: it combined her love of science and animals in an exciting, hands-on profession.

After graduating from veterinary school, Dr. Campbell worked as an intern for a year and subsequently accepted a five-year residency at the University of Pennsylvania Veterinary Hospital. There she gained specialized training in small-animal emergency and critical care medicine as well as anesthesia. Today she shares ER duties with Dr. Hackett at Colorado State's Veterinary Teaching Hospital, where she's an assistant professor.

One aspect Dr. Campbell especially enjoys about working at the hospital is teaming with doctors to solve animal medical mysteries. "It's easy to do here because everybody loves to take the team approach and respects each other's specialties," she says. "Everyone

Growing up in Medford, Oregon, Dr. Vicki Campbell loved animals, including her cocker spaniel named Angel. Like most ER vets, she enjoys the work's exciting ups and downs. Maybe that's why one of her favorite hobbies to this day is riding roller coasters!

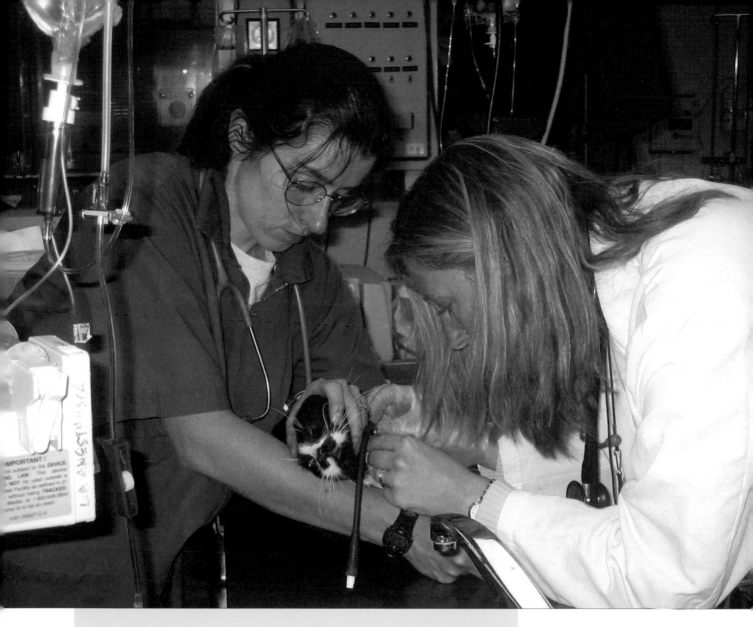

constantly wants to learn, and sometimes we see such complicated cases that it helps to sit down and pick each other's brain on them."

Dr. Campbell recalls one case involving a cat with an icy-cold right front leg, which doctors thought had a blood clot. "Normally when we see this, it's secondary to heart disease, but the cat's heart was normal. The only abnormality we could find was high blood pressure. So we started him on therapy for a blood clot, and he seemed to get better," she says. "The owners were thrilled and everyone was happy, but three weeks later, the same thing happened with the left front leg.

Saving lives takes teamwork, says Dr. Campbell. Here she works with a student to help this kitten stay alive.

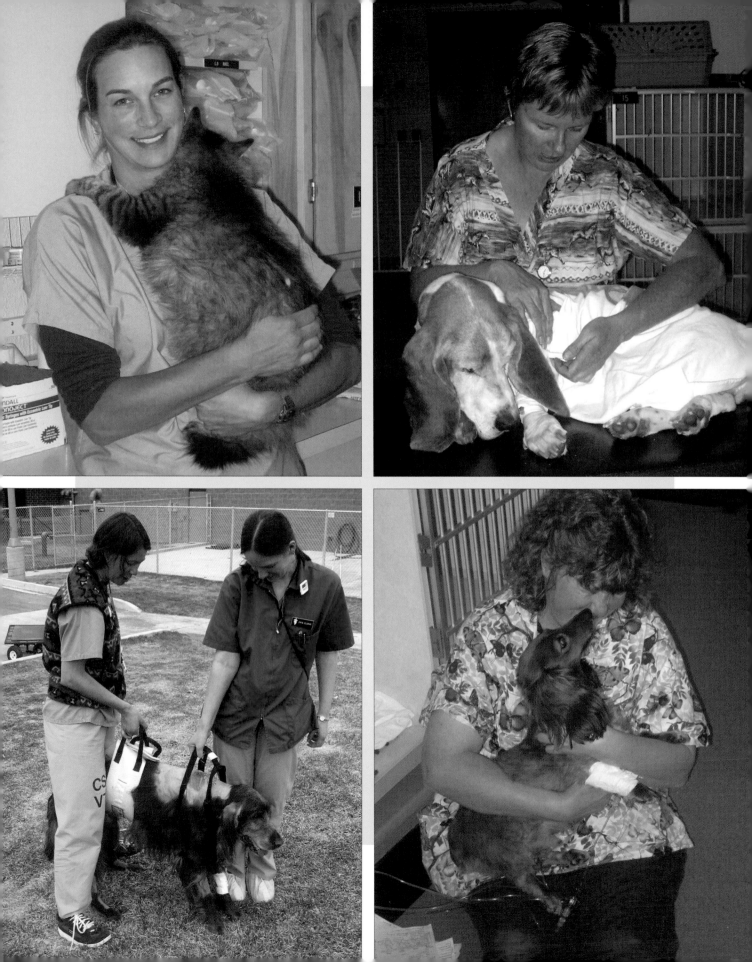

"Nobody had ever seen this before," she says, "and we couldn't explain it since the cat didn't have heart disease." After talking to everyone in the hospital and running more diagnostic tests, doctors discovered a tumor in the cat's lung that they believe caused little bits of tissue to lodge into the cat's legs. Sadly, the cat died a few weeks later.

That's the frustrating and emotionally draining part of the job, says Dr. Campbell. "But for the animals that you do save, there's no other feeling like it. It's not just saving the life of the patient," she says. "It's how happy a family—mom, dad, and children—will be when their pet comes home."

ER VETERINARY TECHNICIANS

Saving lives takes a team effort, says Dr. Campbell. "Especially when a really sick patient comes in. And by far the most important members of the team are the veterinary technicians [also referred to as nurses and vet techs]," she says.

Nurses often make "the first-call triage decisions for patients," explains ER nurse Brenda Francis. "In a GDV [bloat] case, for example, we'll start IV fluids and get everything in line so the doctor can place a tube into the dog's stomach. At the same time, we walk students through the procedure, telling them what we're doing and why."

When patients require intensive care after surgery, veterinary technicians remain close by—just in case an animal's condition takes a turn for the worse. They check vital signs, dispense medications, monitor pain and comfort levels, and join animals in their cages to offer reassuring hugs.

"Vets solve the mysteries of an animal's illness," says ER nurse Sue Mordi, but nurses put their hands around the patients twenty-four hours a day. "That's what I like about being a nurse," says the former pre-vet student. "It's intuitive and hands-on."

Veterinary technicians come from a variety of backgrounds, but the majority earn a two- or four-year degree through a program accredited by the American Veterinary Medical Association (AVMA). Most states also require technicians to pass an exam to become certified, licensed, or registered to practice.

Veterinary technicians—or nurses—are the backbone of the ER team. They "put their hands around" patients and ensure that animals receive individualized care and constant monitoring. Many veterinary technicians (and doctors) adopt animals that come through the ER who would otherwise be put to sleep.

FACING PAGE, CLOCKWISE FROM UPPER LEFT:

Vet tech Brenda Francis hugs her pet cat, Delilah.

Vet tech Cheryl Spencer checks a bassett hound's temperature.

Vet tech Laura Kelly enjoys an affectionate moment with a long-haired dachshund.

Vet tech Sue Mordi and a student walk an Irish setter that's had back surgery.

FACING PAGE, TOP:
Vet tech Jocey Pronko washes a poodle.

FACING PAGE, BOTTOM:
Resident vet Dr. Jacqueline Whittemore calculates the amount of medicine to administer to her canine patient, as vet tech Brenda Francis awaits the final number.

A vet tech's responsibilities include everything from assisting in medical and surgical procedures to collecting specimens, performing lab tests, and taking x-rays. Some specialize in specific areas of medicine, such as anesthesiology and emergency and critical care.

"Nurses are patient advocates," says Leslie Carter, the ER's head nurse. "We see the subtle changes in a patient's condition, and we're always thinking: 'How can I make this better? How can I collaborate with the doctor to make sure we're doing everything possible for the animal's pain?'"

Working closely with the animals makes the job worthwhile for most vet techs, but it can be heartbreaking when things don't go well. "We had this cool Doberman pinscher that kept eating foreign objects, and I got really attached to him," says ER nurse Stephanie Pitzer. "We spent a week trying everything we could to fix him, but he didn't have enough intestine left [after all his ER visits] and his body just gave out. It was horribly sad," she says.

"Nurses take it personally when they lose a patient," explains Carter. "We always wonder if there was something else we could have done." At times, nurses struggle with pet owners' decisions—especially when animals appear to suffer needlessly as a result.

"The most discouraging cases are those where you know in your heart an animal doesn't have a chance of making it, but the owners can't let go," says Pitzer. "They keep pushing treatments, because they have the money to do so."

One way nurses—and the rest of the ER team—work off stress is through humor. Finbar, a sweet but smelly golden retriever, passed a lot of gas during his stay at the ER, providing days of comic relief.

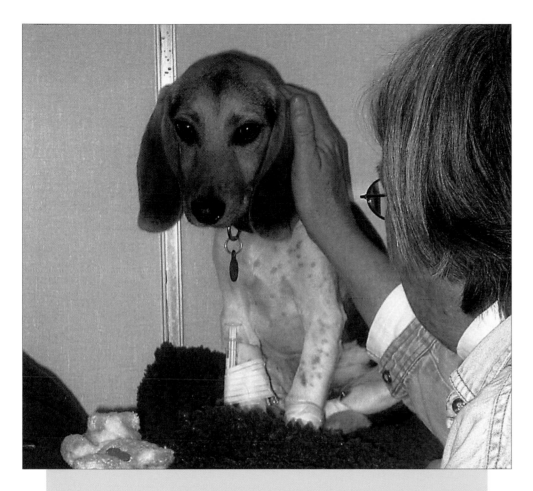

Despite the emotional demands, ER veterinary technicians love their jobs. "Not a day goes by that I don't learn something new," says ER nurse Amy Mayhak. "Each case is unique, as well as each shift." During the day, there's lots of people contact, she says. At night, the hospital halls are quiet, but more emergencies rush through—especially after veterinary clinics close and people come home from work. "By midnight, the pace becomes more laid back, and you have more time for patient care."

Cheryl Spencer has worked all the shifts in her more than twenty-five years as a vet tech and has witnessed many changes in veterinary medicine since beginning her career. "When I first started, dogs and cats were considered more disposable," she says. "People looked at you a little funny if you thought of your pet as a family member." Ninety-five percent of vets also were men, she says. Today, women comprise 75 percent of the field.

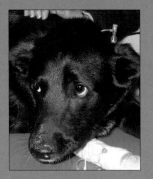

The Chaknova family adopted Shelley from a shelter in Denver. She's always been a sweet dog, they say.

SHELLEY: HBC

"**d**OG HIT BY CAR."

Animal Control Officer Brandy Perkins picked up the call on her way home from work and immediately headed toward the scene of the accident.

"When I arrived, there was a man kneeling on the ground with a blanket over a dog and two golden retrievers sitting in the man's Chevy Suburban," she says. Apparently, all three of the dogs ran across the road and were struck by the vehicle, with "Shelley"—an eleven-month-old border collie mix—taking the brunt of the hit.

"Shelley was in shock," says Perkins, whose job is to investigate cases involving abused or injured animals in Boulder County, Colorado. "She had visible injuries on her mouth and blood dripping from her nose. Her breathing was extremely fast and heavy, and things didn't look very good. . . . I wasn't sure she had a chance."

Perkins and the driver of the car carefully moved Shelley to the front seat of the animal control truck and loaded the golden retrievers—both of whom appeared to be in good condition—in the back. "Then I jumped in, put Shelley's head on my lap and headed for the Animal Emergency Center in Longmont. My goal was to get there as fast as I could."

STABILIZING SHELLEY

At the clinic, ER vet Dr. Jacob Head quickly assessed the situation and checked Shelley's vital signs: breathing, temperature, heart rate,

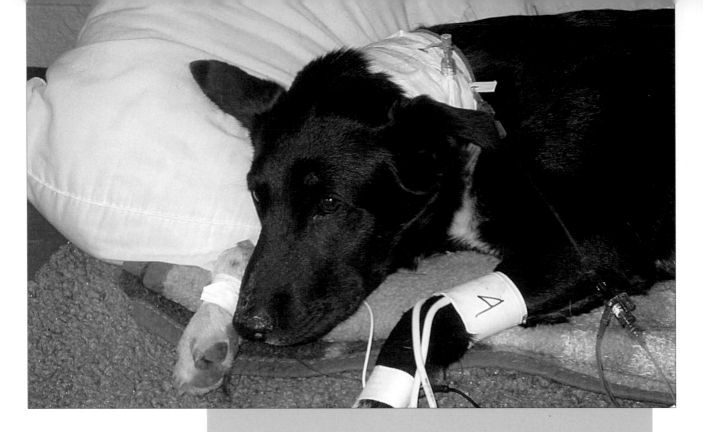

and blood pressure. "Shelley was in severe shock," he says. Her pale gums, rapid heartbeat, and low blood pressure signaled inadequate blood flow as well as a lack of oxygen, which if left untreated could result in death. Shelley's pelvis was also painful, and she couldn't walk, says Dr. Head.

X-rays revealed that Shelley suffered from, among other injuries, a severe fracture to her left femur (thigh bone) as well as bruised and collapsed lungs. To stabilize her condition, the ER vet administered IV fluids, oxygen, and pain medication. "We work to get the major organs and systems going again," explains Dr. Head. "Then we evaluate conditions that are not life-threatening, such as broken bones."

Back at David and Jane Chaknova's house, all was quiet. Too quiet. "We came home, and there was no Shelley," says David Chaknova. A message on the answering machine soon solved the mystery. It was Brandy Perkins from Animal Control, saying that Shelley was at the emergency center and was in "rough shape."

The Chaknovas hurried to the clinic.

"This is a sweet dog," Dr. Head told the family. "If we can keep her stable, her injuries can be repaired."

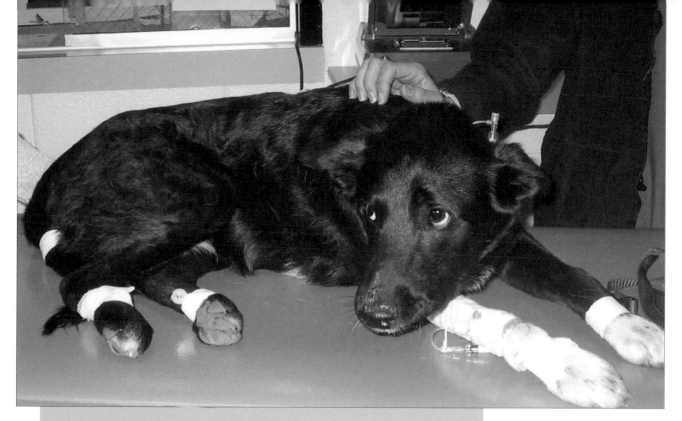

David Chaknova called Shelley's regular veterinarian, Dr. Steve Benscheidt, and showed him the dog's x-rays. Given Shelley's fragile condition and the orthopedic (skeletal) surgery involved, he recommended the family take their dog to veterinary specialists at Colorado State University. The next day, David Chaknova drove Shelley to the vet hospital, where ER vets awaited her arrival.

RECHECKING THE PUP

"The first thing we did was to reevaluate her condition," explains Dr. Michael Walters, a third-year resident specializing in emergency medicine at Colorado State's veterinary hospital. "We took chest rads [x-rays] so that we could take another look at her lungs and the pneumothorax." (A pneumothorax is a collapsed lung caused by air trapped in the space between the lungs and chest wall, which interferes with breathing.) "The lungs are more important to me than a fracture," says Dr. Walters. "Animals won't die from a fracture or a broken bone; they'll die because their heart or lungs aren't working well."

The x-rays showed continued evidence of a collapsed and bruised left lung. "Bruised lungs affect how well an animal's bloodstream can get oxygen and let carbon dioxide out," explains Dr. Walters. Shelley

After being hit by a car, Shelley needed orthopedic surgery to repair hip and thigh fractures so she could walk again. Before proceeding with the operation, ER vets confirmed that she was ready by ordering x-rays and blood tests to rule out any abnormalities.

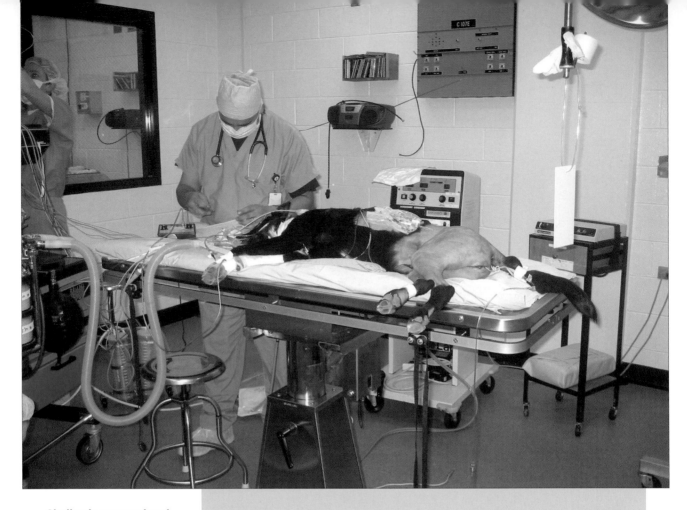

Shelley is prepped and ready for surgery at Colorado State University's Veterinary Teaching Hospital.

also had an abnormal heartbeat—called an arrhythmia—"which is not uncommon after a chest trauma," he says. "Not only can the lungs bruise, but the heart can bruise as well."

To ensure that Shelley's body could handle surgery to repair her hip and thigh fractures, doctors prescribed IV fluids, oxygen, and drugs to control her heart rhythm. An electrocardiogram (ECG) also monitored the electrical activity of her heart through the night. The next morning, Shelley appeared more alert. A second set of lung x-rays and a complete blood count (CBC) to rule out abnormalities of the red blood cells, white blood cells, and platelets (cells that help blood to clot) helped confirm that she was ready for surgery.

MAJOR REPAIRS

Before wheeling Shelley into the operating room, nurses prepped her with IV tubes for fluids and probes for monitoring her vital signs. One probe, connected to a device called a pulse oximeter, was

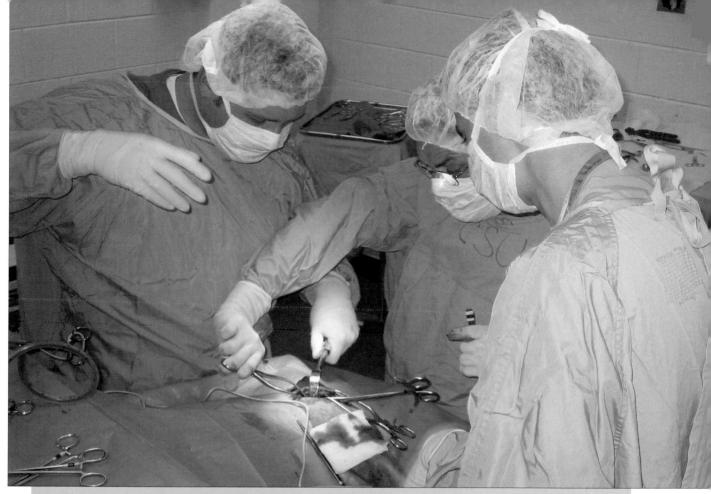

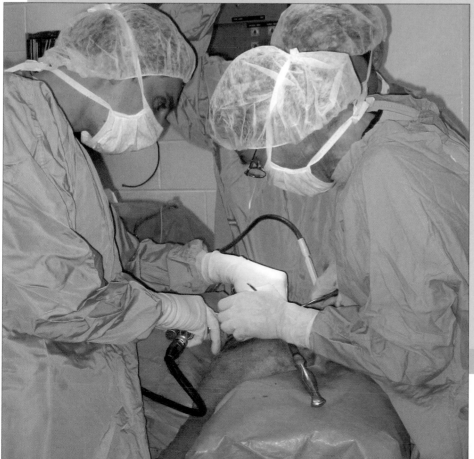

Surgeons, led by
Dr. Erick Egger,
spent about five
hours carefully
mending Shelley's
bones.

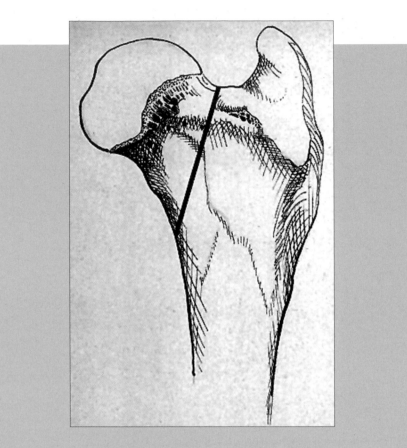

clipped to her tongue to measure the oxygen saturation of her blood. Nurses also placed a breathing tube in Shelley's windpipe (trachea) so she could inhale a gas anesthetic, which would put her into a deep sleep during the operation and prevent her from feeling pain.

Soon after, veterinary students shaved Shelley's lower body so it could be sterilized with antiseptic soap and alcohol. Protecting the patient from infection during surgery is a top priority. For this reason, everything is kept sterile, from the operating room to the stainless steel surgical instruments. Doctors and nurses stay germ-free, as well. Before each operation, they put on sterile surgical gowns, caps, gloves, face masks, and shoe covers and vigorously scrub bacteria from their hands, fingernails, and forearms.

Shelley's surgery lasted about five hours. "We repaired and stabilized the right pelvic [hip] fracture with a steel plate and screws," explains orthopedic surgeon Dr. Erick Egger. As for the left side, two areas needed repair: the ball portion of the hip joint, which was fractured at the growth layer between the cap of the ball and the socket,

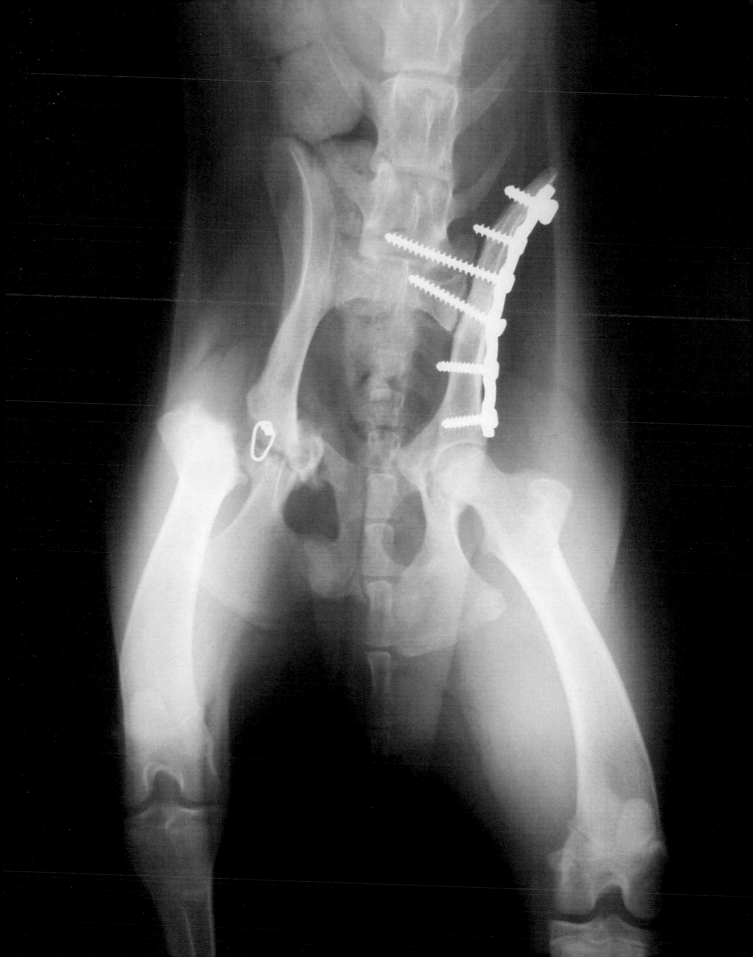

ABOVE: **Six days after surgery, Shelley returned home to her family. From left, David, Jane, Marcus, and Rachel Chaknova with Shelley.**

FACING PAGE: **Four months after being hit by a car, Shelley reunites with Dr. Jacob Head— the ER vet who initially treated her at the Animal Emergency Center in Longmont.**

cutting off its blood supply and preventing it from healing; and the cup-shaped socket that receives the ball portion of the joint, which was fractured.

To give Shelley "the most functional limb possible," surgeons performed a femoral head ostectomy, or FHO. "We took the ball portion of the hip joint out," says Dr. Egger. "This allows her to form a false joint that will be held together with scar tissue and muscles supporting it. It will no longer be a bone and cartilage joint—it will be a scar tissue and muscle joint." As for the socket fracture, doctors stabilized it using orthopedic wire to hold it together.

Six days after surgery, Shelley returned home to her family to begin recovery. "For weeks, her hip and upper thigh were swollen and painful," says David Chaknova. But Shelley's drive to be active—paired with the Chaknova family's efforts to rehabilitate their dog by progressively increasing her exercise—helped her bones heal and grow strong. "It took a couple of months before she really started using her left leg," says David Chaknova. "Now she's chasing rabbits and birds again."

toxic treats

Killer grapes? Poisonous onions? Deadly chunks of chocolate?

Surprising, but true—if you're a dog or a cat.

"Chocolate contains a stimulant called theobromine, which can cause heart problems and be toxic in sufficient quantities," says ER vet Dr. Michael Walters. Dark baker's chocolate is the most dangerous. "A small dog weighing five to twenty pounds can die from eating one half to two ounces of baker's chocolate." Milk chocolate also can be lethal, but more is needed to harm a dog or cat because it contains a lower concentration of stimulants per ounce.

Signs that your pet may have eaten harmful amounts of chocolate include restlessness, hyperactivity, vomiting, diarrhea, muscle tremors, and seizures. In severe cases, it may even slip into a coma. "Call your vet immediately if you suspect your pet has eaten chocolate," advises Dr. Walters.

Grapes and raisins—once considered healthy training treats—also can be fatal to dogs by causing kidney failure, although the toxic component is still unknown. Dogs that become sick from eating grapes and raisins typically vomit within a few hours, lose their appetites, develop diarrhea, become lethargic, and suffer abdominal pain. Symptoms last from a few days to several weeks. If left unchecked, damage to the kidneys progresses until a dog is unable to produce urine and dies.

Fortunately, early treatment can prevent kidney damage, explains Dr. Charlotte Means, a veterinary toxicologist at the American Society for the Prevention of Cruelty to Animals (ASPCA) Animal Poison Control Center. Inducing vomiting and giving a dog activated charcoal—an antidote that soaks up poisons from the stomach and intestines—helps prevent potential toxins from inflicting damage. Dr. Means also recommends hospitalizing dogs so vets can monitor their condition.

Other foods that may harm animals include

- Onions, which contain an ingredient called thiosulphate that can destroy red blood cells and cause severe anemia

Chocolate contains a stimulant that can cause heart problems and even death in pets.

- avocados, which can cause breathing difficulties and death in small birds
- macadamia nuts, which may cause temporary vomiting, diarrhea, lethargy, and paralysis in dogs
- fatty foods, which can give pets pancreatitis — a painful swelling of the pancreas

To learn more about animal poison control, visit the American Society for the Prevention of Cruelty to Animals (ASPCA) Animal Poison Control Center Web site, which is located off the main site at www.aspca.org, or contact them at 1-888-426-4435.

Lucy Slips Away

Michelle Strong loved Lucy from the moment she saw her. For years she'd longed for a pet snake, and now she finally had one. A gentle, two-pound ball python, Lucy glistened in her hunter green skin that was accented with brown, mushroom-shaped markings.

Ball pythons, also known as royal pythons in the United Kingdom, originate from West Africa and grow to be three to five feet long. They're crepuscular—active during the twilight periods of dawn and dusk—and are generally shy and reluctant to bite. In fact, they're called ball pythons because they curl their bodies into a tight ball when nervous or threatened.

Michelle and her husband, Adam, pampered Lucy. They bought her a fifty-five-gallon tank that they furnished with coconut-fiber down (organic dirt) for bedding, bamboo sticks for her to climb, a water bowl, and a hiding log that she could tuck her body all the way under—something ball pythons love to do.

As the months passed, Lucy doubled in size and became an integral part of the Strong family. Even the family's cat, Matilda, tolerated her. Life seemed fine until February 2004 when Michelle noticed a few scabs on Lucy's skin. Worried about her health, Michelle

Ball pythons curl them-selves into a ball when nervous or threatened.

brought Lucy to the veterinarian on the afternoon of February 12. Fortunately, Lucy's condition wasn't serious—most likely cuts from her hiding log, concluded the doctor, who sent Michelle home with some cream.

INTO THIN AIR

After leaving the vet's office at four p.m., Michelle placed Lucy in a pillowcase and rested the snake on the front passenger's seat next to her. "I didn't tie the pillowcase in a knot," says Michelle, "because we had done this many times before, and she would just lie there and curl into a ball." When Michelle arrived home twenty minutes later, she discovered the pillowcase was empty. Where was Lucy?

Michelle searched the car for her snake, but to no avail. Most likely, she concluded, Lucy had slithered behind the dashboard. Now what?

"I panicked because it was unusually cold that night," she says, and snakes thrive in warm temperatures. "So I called the pet store for advice. They told me to try to lure her out with the warmth of a heating pad and by putting a mouse in a container with holes on the top so Lucy could smell it. They also advised keeping the doors closed and leaving everything quiet so I didn't scare her back up the dash."

Michelle followed the instructions, peeking through the car windows every few hours during the night to see if Lucy surfaced. But she never did.

Michelle Strong let Lucy slither around the house—always keeping a close eye on her.

Early the next morning, Michelle rushed to a car dealership and asked the mechanics if they would look for Lucy behind the dashboard. At first they refused, worried that Lucy might bite. But after some reassurance and a few tears from Michelle, they pulled out the glove compartment and dismantled the dash. When Michelle peered behind the dashboard, she immediately saw Lucy, camouflaged among the hoses. Unfortunately, it would take one more trip to a specialty car dealership before Michelle could retrieve Lucy, place her in a box, and rush her to the veterinary hospital.

"When I arrived, I saw a vet standing outside taking a break, so I threw the box in his arms and said, 'I think she's dead, please help me!'"

The vet rushed Lucy to the emergency room.

Meanwhile, back in the waiting area, an exhausted Michelle dissolved into tears. *Why didn't I tie a knot in the pillowcase?* she thought. *Why did I wait until morning to go to the dealership?* Suddenly, Michelle felt a hand on her shoulder. It was Gail Bishop, one of the hospital's veterinary grief counselors.

Michelle and Adam Strong pampered Lucy with a hiding log and bamboo to climb. Just like a cat or dog, Lucy became an integral part of the Strong family.

"How's my snake?" Michelle sobbed.

"They're warming her up right now," Gail reassured her. "The doctor will be out to talk with you shortly."

WAITING FOR A SIGN

Dr. Matthew Johnston, who specializes in treating exotic animals such as reptiles, explained the situation.

"When a snake comes in with no heartbeat—which we determine via an ultrasonographic doppler probe—we don't assume that it is dead," he says. "This is especially true when hypothermia [abnormally low body temperature] is the suspected cause, as was the case with Lucy.

"Snakes are cold-blooded—unable to produce their own body heat—and have the ability to slow down their metabolic rate when temperatures get too cold," he says. "The definition of death in reptiles is cessation of the heartbeat for twenty-four hours."

To determine if Lucy was dead or in a hypothermic stupor, Dr. Johnston aggressively worked to rewarm the snake by injecting warm fluids into her body to bathe her internal organs. He also cushioned her with heating pads. Once Lucy reached her preferred optimum temperature zone of 80 to 95 degrees Fahrenheit, he would wait about fifteen minutes to see if a heartbeat developed. "If she doesn't wake up then," he told Michelle, "she won't wake up."

Time ticked away, with Dr. Johnston checking in with Michelle every twenty minutes to let her know Lucy's temperature. After about an hour and a half, Dr. Johnston delivered the sad news: Lucy had died.

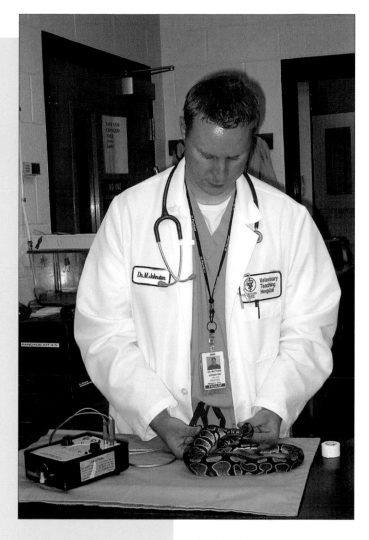

Dr. Matthew Johnston uses an ultrasonographic doppler probe to listen to this snake's heartbeat. This is the same tool he used to listen to Lucy's heart.

With Gail by her side, Michelle said her final goodbyes to Lucy in one of the hospital's comfort rooms. "I took it hard," Michelle remembers. "I blamed myself completely." Gail reminded Michelle that Lucy died accidentally and that her intentions were honorable. "You were taking such great care of this snake," Gail told her, "and that's what you were doing when this happened."

Michelle grieved the death of her pet snake for about a month. "I still had her aquarium set up, and sometimes I'd forget and think she was still there."

"I loved Lucy like you would love a dog or a cat or any other pet you might have," says Michelle. "Gail and Dr. Johnston understood my grief, and that helped me get through it."

deAth of a pet

d isbelief. Anger. Sadness.

The death of a pet hurts our hearts in ways that can be difficult to understand. We grow up with our pets and love them like family members, feeding them when they're hungry and caring for them when they're ill. It's only natural that we would grieve their loss. When death occurs suddenly—as in an accident or other emergency situation—our sorrow can be especially overwhelming.

To support families with critically ill pets, Colorado State's veterinary hospital offers counseling and guidance through its Argus Institute for Families and Veterinary Medicine. "Our focus is on the pet owner," says Gail Bishop, counselor and coordinator of clinical services and community outreach. "Everybody else is focused on the patient first, then the pet owner."

When an emergency case arrives at the hospital, the front desk pages a vet to take the animal to the ER. "They also page a counselor, so that we can immediately meet with the pet owner," says Bishop. "At that point, we generally have a very emotional person with empty arms and an incredible amount of anxiety."

Counselors bring pet owners to a comfortable room and offer them something to drink. "A glass of water, a cup of coffee, and some

While the rest of the veterinary hospital focuses on sick animals, Gail Bishop (center) helps pet owners sort through their emotions when a pet is critically ill or injured.

Deciding what's best for a dying animal can be difficult for families.

tissues are always available," says Bishop. Then they assess the situation: Are the pet owners emotionally ready for what may happen next? Do they have loved ones to help them through the crisis?

When the time is right, the counselor offers to visit the emergency room to learn more about the pet's condition and to see if the

ER vet needs information from the pet owners. "I paint a picture of what's happening in the emergency room to try to lessen pet owners' anxiety," says Bishop. "I can let them know, for instance, that we have our best emergency vets working on their pet and that they have her on oxygen."

Bishop also assists the ER vets and nurses. "They may say: 'This doesn't look good, would you ask the family if they want CPR?' or 'Let's have a student go back with you to get a history and find out what's going on.' If the situation's really bad," says Bishop, "the doctors come out to ask pet owners the tough questions and/or to talk about emergency surgery or diagnostic tests."

Dogs feel emotions, too. A surviving pet may grieve the loss of a companion.

"A GOOD DEATH"

While ER vets work many medical miracles, they can't save every pet. Sometimes an animal dies while it's being treated. Other times, the patient is so severely ill or injured, it's left suffering with no hope of recovery. When this happens, the vet will ask pet owners one of the most difficult questions of all: Would you consider euthanasia—helping your pet to die—as an option?

Euthanasia (pronounced "you-thuh-nay-zhuh") is a Greek word meaning "a good or gentle death." During the procedure, a vet injects an overdose of an anesthetic—the same medicine used to prevent pain in surgery—into an animal, so that it slips into unconsciousness and dies peacefully without pain. Many consider euthanasia a kind or humane way to end a dying animal's unnecessary suffering.

How do you know when it's time to say goodbye?

"It's never easy," according to the Argus Institute's *Family Guide to Pet Loss.* "On one hand, you want your pet to live, but on the other hand, you don't want your pet to suffer. You fear losing your pet and the grief that will follow, but you also fear seeing your pet in pain."

One way counselors help families decide is by asking them to list three things that make their pet who he is. "Since the pet can't tell us, this helps us figure out when he's suffering," explains counselor Bobbie Beach. Will "Max" ever play ball again? Will he eat his favorite treats and chew on his toys? If breathing with a ventilator is all he can do from now on, is this the quality of life that we want for him?

"If not, then we have some control over the quality of his death," says Beach. The vets and his owners can help him die peacefully and honor him by saying goodbye and celebrating his life. It's important to remember that "*we're* not killing the animal—the injury or disease is killing him," says Beach. "We're helping him die so he doesn't suffer."

When a family decides that euthanasia is the best choice, they may choose to be present for their pet's final moments and share memories of their lives together. Some bring other family pets. "It may seem difficult to be with pets when they die," says Beach, "but with appropriate emotional support, it can be a positive experience that eases the grieving process."

DEALING WITH DEATH

Grieving the death of a pet is a sad but normal healing response to our loss. It's also a complicated one. Each of us reacts differently depending on factors such as our age, personality, attachment to our pet, and the circumstances surrounding death.

At first, we may feel numb and deny that our pet is gone. When reality sinks in, we may cry when we see our pet's empty water bowl, snap at friends who don't understand our pain, or feel guilty for not doing more to save our companion's life. To cope with our tangled emotions, some of us spend time alone and temporarily withdraw from activities. Others keep very busy. During this time, it's especially important to talk about our feelings with people we trust, say counselors. This is particularly important if it's our first experience with death, because we may need extra support in sorting out our emotions.

Other healthy ways to express our thoughts include keeping a

One way to express emotions after the death of a pet is to create art. One of nine-year-old Kyle's favorite memories of his dog Bingo is how he used to jump on him and lick his face. When Bingo died, Kyle hugged him and said goodbye. After some time, he cried and remembered two other pets who had died—Bubba, a parakeet, and Rocket, a cockatiel. "Bubba used to fly on top of my head and make me laugh," Kyle says. "I miss Bubba and Bingo and so does [my brother] Sean."

journal, designing a scrapbook, creating art, or writing a story, poem, or song. Planting a tree or garden in honor of our pet may also provide comfort. Many times, helping others—including our surviving pets—deal with their grief makes us feel better. "Animals form attachments to other animals and may become upset when separated from them," says Beach. Signs that a pet is grieving include nervousness, lethargy, clinginess, loss of appetite, and trouble sleeping. Keeping a pet's daily routine as normal as possible and engaging in everyday activities, such as walking, has benefits for everyone, says Beach.

In time, the intensity of our loss lessens and we may be ready to welcome another pet into our lives.

RAISING CAIN

MARCH 27, 2004

The signal went off at five a.m. Peek-a-Boon—a prized mare —was ready to give birth. Nikki Cain and her husband, Matt, rushed to the barn at the Double Dove Ranch. When they arrived two minutes later, their eyes immediately fell on the tiny foal in front of them.

"He was really little, lying in a fetal position—and he was blue," says Nikki. Immediately, she and her husband positioned the foal so that his head was upright, then gave him oxygen. "At that point, I didn't think he had a chance," says Nikki. "He was so weak and frail that when we lifted him he folded in half."

All at once, the foal breathed on his own—tiny, shallow breaths —but breaths revealing that he wanted to live. "That's when I knew he had a chance," says Nikki. "It still didn't look good, but he had a chance."

6:30 A.M. NEONATAL INTENSIVE CARE UNIT

The foal arrived at Colorado State's veterinary hospital an hour and a half after birth, extremely cold and weak. "He needed critical care or else he was going to die," says Dr. Darien Feary, a resident vet specializing in equine (horse-related) internal medicine. "He also needed a nickname so everyone would fight for him," says Gina Gonzales, nursing coordinator for the neonatal intensive care unit for foals. "If he has a name it's harder for us to let go."

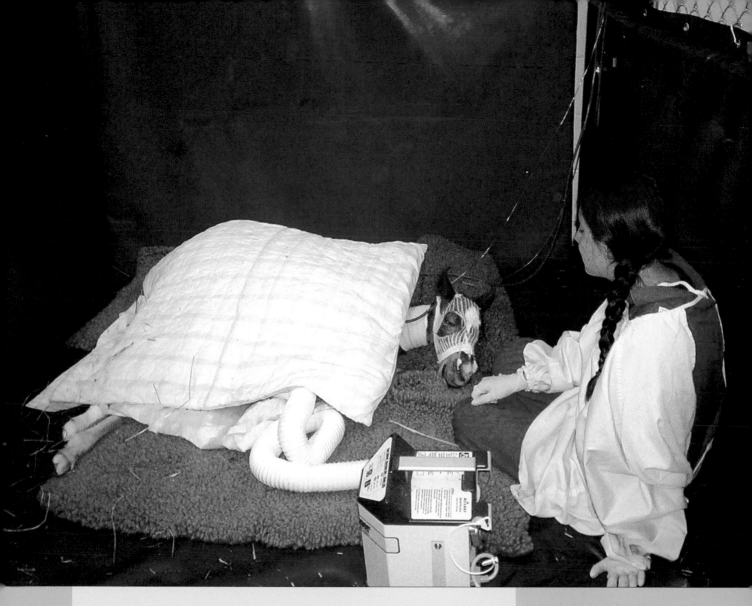

With the owner's permission, the large-animal team gave "the full-on emergency treatment" to the foal, now nicknamed "Paco the Taco" for the way he looked in a Hug-U-Vac positioning system that kept him upright so he could breathe.

"We put him on [nasal] oxygen right away and did blood work," explains Dr. Feary. While awaiting blood test results, they warmed Paco with an air blanket and administered IV fluids because he was dehydrated. Since Paco hadn't nursed yet, they placed a tube inside his stomach to feed him his mother's colostrum—a fluid rich in antibodies that a mare produces just before and after giving birth. Eventually, nurses replaced the colostrum feedings with his mother's milk.

"Paco the Taco," nicknamed by nurses, rests in an air blanket that keeps him warm. Paco weighed about 60 pounds when he was born. Most cutting horses—those trained to round up cattle—weigh from 80 to 150 pounds at birth.

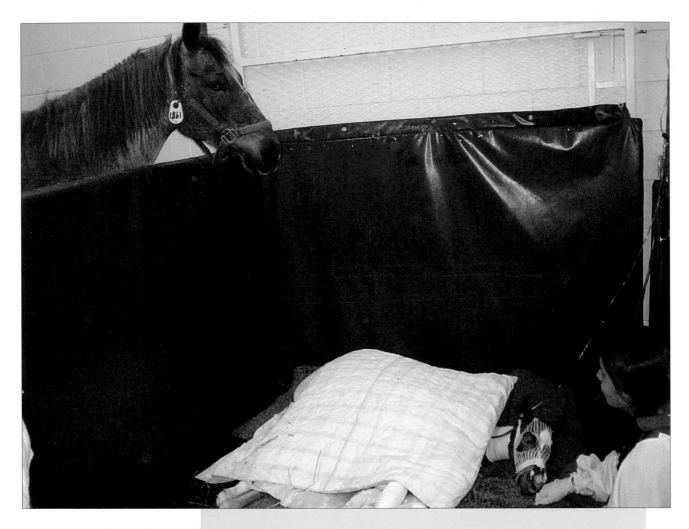

Paco's mother, Peek-a-Boon, checks on her newborn foal soon after they arrive at the vet hospital.

Blood tests revealed multiple problems for Paco—all associated with a lack of oxygen and nutrients before he was born. The diagnosis? Hypoxic-ischemic encephalopathy, also referred to as "dummy foal syndrome." "Hypoxia means not enough oxygen is reaching organs, such as the brain—which is why a foal may act 'dumb' initially," says Dr. Feary. "But it also affects other organs, such as the kidneys, liver, and heart. So he had a widespread, multiorgan lack of oxygen."

"Years ago, he would have died from this," says Dr. Feary. "But in the past decade, we've found that hypoxic injuries can be completely reversed. Once foals pull through it, there's no reason to think they won't be normal."

The question was, would Paco pull through?

With a diagnosis in hand, doctors aggressively treated Paco with antibiotics and other medications. Experience also led them to anticipate problems associated with the syndrome, such as seizures, which can be severe and further complicate matters. Sure enough, two days after Paco arrived at the hospital, he suffered seizures. To control them, Dr. Hackett from the small-animal emergency room recommended midazolam, a drug doctors use to treat human premature babies. The medicine sedated Paco and stopped his seizures so that his brain would have time to heal. Multiple hurdles remained, however.

CRUCIAL PERIOD

About this time, senior vet student Mandy Chandler met her new three-day-old patient. "When I first saw him, he was in a coma and completely unresponsive to anything," she says. "I'd come in and talk to him and touch him, but he didn't respond. It looked pretty bad."

Doctors sedated Paco with a drug used on human babies when he began to suffer seizures.

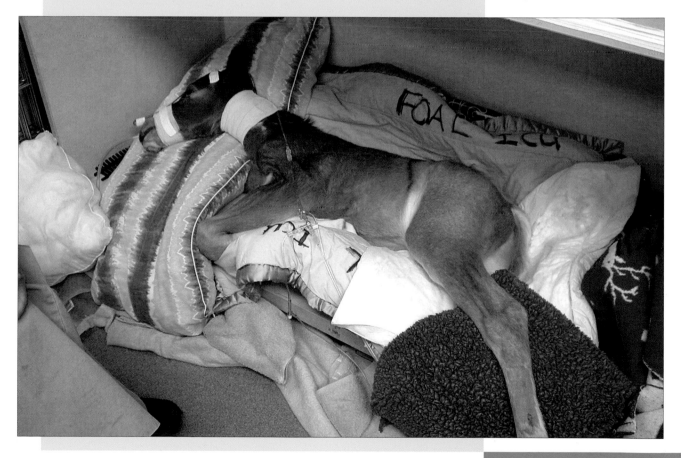

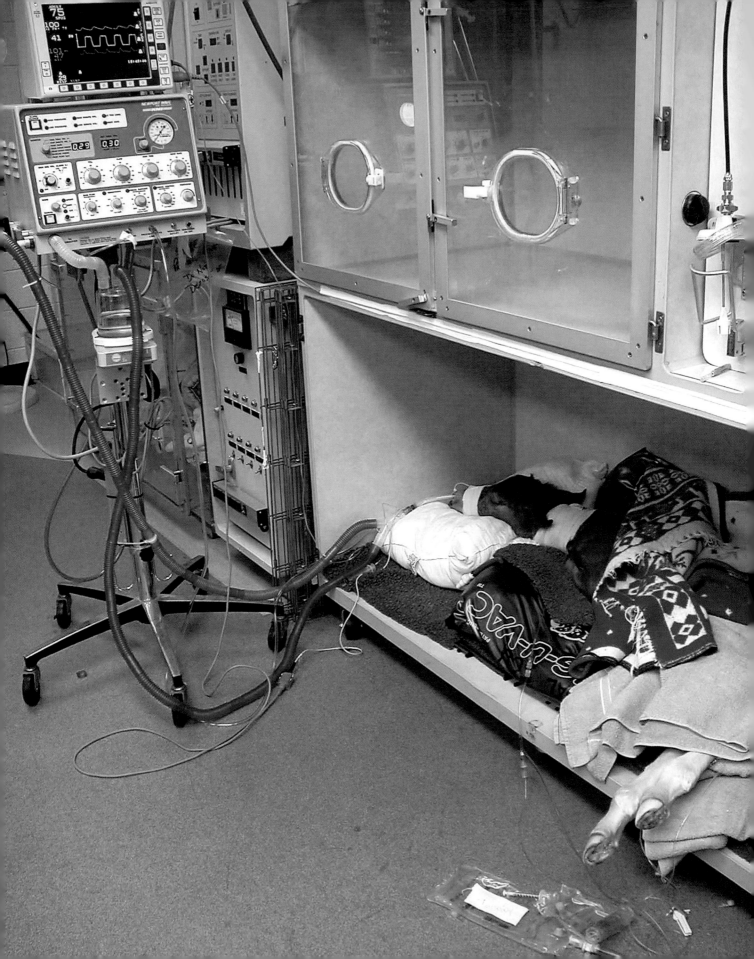

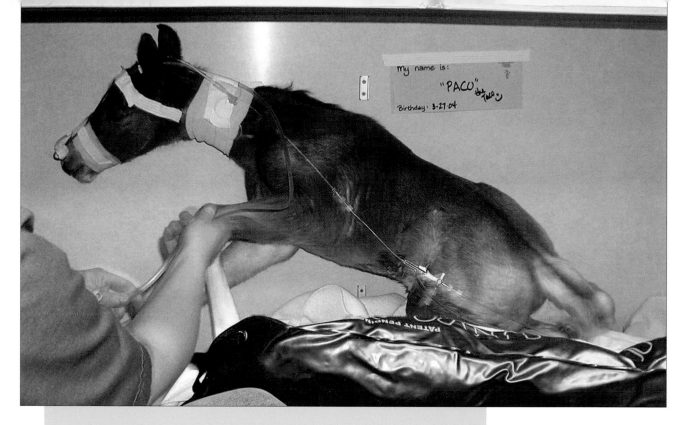

Dr. Feary didn't like the look of things either. Though she had Paco on nasal oxygen, his lungs just weren't doing their job, and it appeared that he was developing pneumonia. Perhaps putting him on a mechanical ventilator would open his airways. So she transferred Paco to the small-animal ER, where Dr. Hackett and resident vet Dr. Heather Connally worked to reexpand the foal's lungs. The move paid off. After eighteen hours, doctors removed Paco from the ventilator and he breathed on his own. Now it was time to wean him from his medications and ask him to wake up and act like a foal.

"This is the crucial moment," Dr. Feary told the ranch's veterinarian, Dr. Judy Merriott. "If he starts to seize again when we bring him out of the coma, then we're back at square one." Fortunately, Paco "opened his eyes, wiggled his ears, and looked around as if to say, 'Where am I?'" No seizures—a very good sign.

Not long afterward, doctors and nurses helped Paco stand on his feet and balance himself. Mother and child also reunited. "Some mares reject their baby after being away from it for a few days," says Mandy, "but Peek-a-Boon didn't. When Paco was wheeled back—all huffing and puffing with his little tail wagging—she nickered at him real low, as if to say, 'That's my baby.'"

ABOVE: Once Paco could breathe on his own, doctors began weaning him from his medicine so that he could begin acting like a "normal" foal.

FACING PAGE: When Paco's lungs weren't doing their job and he began to develop pneumonia, doctors transferred him to the small-animal ER so he could breathe with the help of a ventilator.

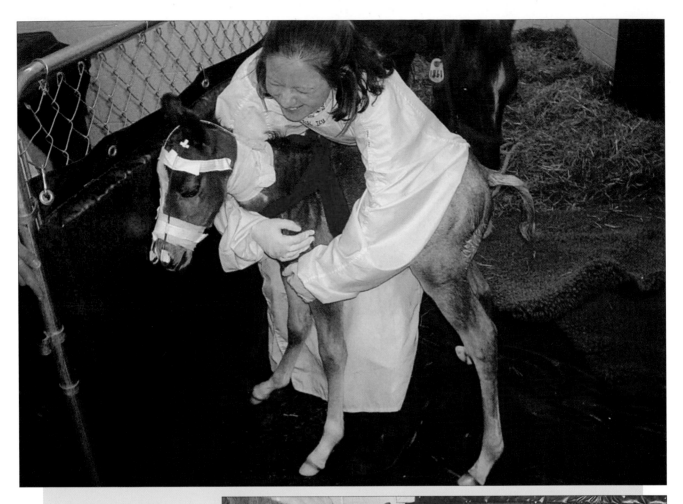

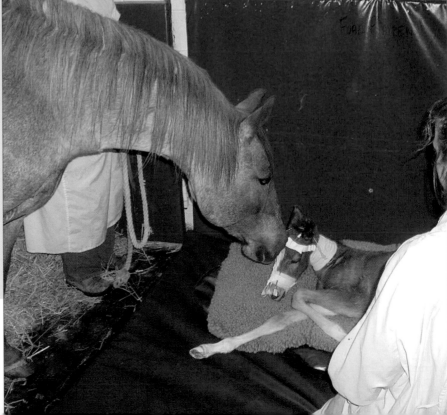

ABOVE: A hospital volunteer helps Paco learn how to stand for the first time since he was born.

RIGHT: The neonatal intensive care team took great care to ensure that Paco and his mother, Peek-a-Boon, remained bonded while he was sick.

FACING PAGE: It wasn't long before Paco walked on his own and learned to nurse.

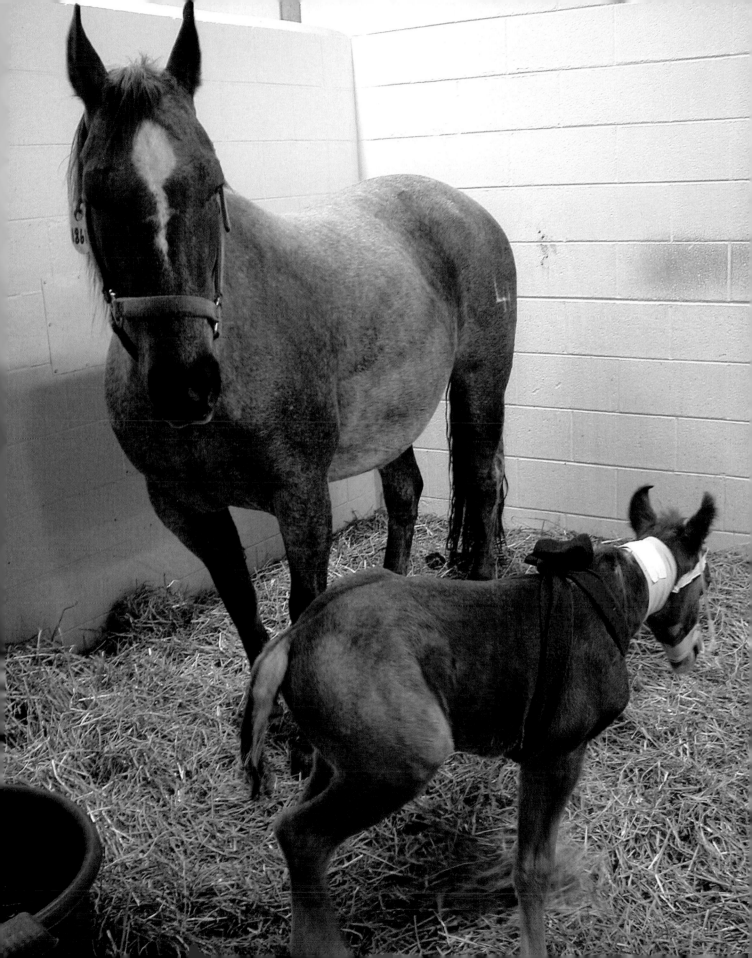

Soon Paco learned to nurse from his mother, and he shed all the tubes that kept him alive during his fragile first few days of life. "I knew he was ready to go home when I went into the stall and had to wrestle him to give him his medicine," says Mandy.

Today the foal — officially named "Reysin Cain" after Nikki Cain, the trainer who tended to him at birth — is a healthy handful who shows no signs of breathing problems or other issues. "He seems as bright and smart and quick and strong as any other horse I have," says owner Gail Holmes. Adds Dr. Merriott, "He truly is a miracle."

pet first-aid kit

Want to handle accidents and medical emergencies as cool and calmly as an ER vet? One way to boost your confidence is to prepare *before* trouble occurs. Having a first-aid kit filled with the proper medical supplies makes it easier to respond quickly when your pet suddenly becomes ill or injured. Many pet stores sell first-aid kits that you can customize, or you may want to build one specifically for your pets. Below are some essential items to include in your kit so that you can treat minor injuries or stabilize your pet's condition until you see the veterinarian.

PET EMERGENCY NUMBERS: Keep a 3″ x 5″ card with the phone numbers of your regular vet, your local poison control center, and the nearest twenty-four-hour emergency animal hospital or clinic. Contact your vet immediately if your pet is sick or seriously injured.

BANDAGES: gauze pads to cushion injuries, and gauze rolls to wrap wounds and stabilize joints

ADHESIVE TAPE: to secure bandages

SCISSORS: preferably with blunt ends, to cut bandages and tape, as well as to clip hair from around wounds

TWEEZERS: to remove ticks, splinters, and other foreign objects from the skin

THERMOMETER: digital works well. Temperature should be taken from the armpit (the axillary region), and you'll need to add one degree for accuracy.

ANTISEPTIC SOLUTION: for cleaning wounds

ANTIBIOTIC CREAM OR OINTMENT: stops bacteria from growing and reduces the risk of infection

TONGUE DEPRESSORS: can be used as splints, especially to stabilize a bird's fractured wing or leg while you transport it to the vet

EYEDROPPER: to give oral medicine

MUZZLE: to prevent dogs from biting. Gauze or nylon stockings can be used as well. Caution: Do not muzzle a dog that's vomiting or having difficulties breathing.

TOWELS: to wrap frightened animals, such as cats, and prevent them from scratching

BLANKETS: to keep your pet warm

GLOVES: to protect your hands and keep contaminants out of open wounds

EMERGENCY ICE PACK: for insect stings or burns. (Do not place directly on a wound—wrap a towel around the wound first.)

COTTON SWABS: for cleaning wounds

TUBE SOCKS: to place over an injured paw

NEWSPAPER, STICKS: to splint a fracture

PENLIGHT: to examine a pet's eyes. (Be sure to pack a couple of extra batteries.)

PET FIRST-AID GUIDE: to provide instructions until you see the vet

WATERPROOF CONTAINER WITH A SECURE TOP: to hold all these items

Warning:
Acetaminophen can kill cats, while ibuprofen may cause kidney failure in dogs. Never give people medication to pets unless a veterinarian prescribes it.

To learn more about pet first aid, contact your local Humane Society. The American Red Cross also offers first-aid courses through its local chapters. Call 1-800-422-7677 for more information.

probing for more?

PUBLICATIONS

Crisp, Marty. *Everything Dog: What Kids Really Want to Know About Dogs (Kids' FAQs)*. Chanhassen, Minn.: NorthWord Press, 2003.

Croke, Vicki, and the Tufts University School of Veterinary Medicine. *Animal ER: Extraordinary Stories of Hope and Healing*. New York: Plume Books, 2000.

Evans, Mark. *Birds: ASPCA Pet Care Guides for Kids*. New York: Dorling Kindersley Books, 2001.

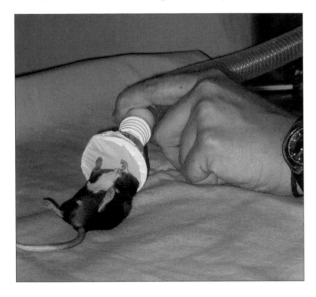

Manning, David. *Keeping Snakes: A Practical Guide to Caring for Unusual Pets*. Hauppauge, N.Y.: Barron's Educational Series, 2001.

Maze Productions. *I Want to Be . . . a Veterinarian*. San Diego: Harcourt Brace & Company, 1997.

Rock, Maxine. *Totally Fun Things to Do with Your Cat (Play with Your Pet)*. New York: John Wiley & Sons, 1998.

Sjonger, Rebecca, and Bobbie Kalman. *Hamsters*. New York: Crabtree Publishing Company, 2004.

Wolfelt, Alan. *Healing Your Grieving Heart for Kids*. Fort Collins, Colo.: Companion Press, 2001.

WEB SITES

American Veterinary Medical Association— Care for Animals: www.avma.org/careforanimals

Argus Institute for Families and Veterinary Medicine: www.argusinstitute.colostate.edu

Colorado State University—James L. Voss Veterinary Teaching Hospital: www.csuvets.colostate.edu

Discovery's Animal Planet: www.animal. discovery.com

Veterinary Emergency and Critical Care Society (VECCS), includes a list of ER hospitals: www.veccs.org

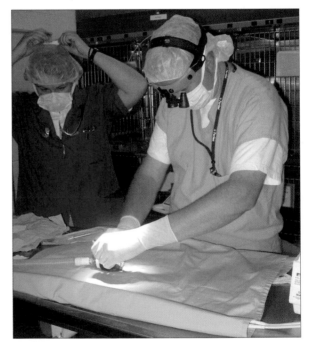

Mouse surgery: When a student discovered that his pet mouse was a he instead of a she, he had the mouse neutered at the hospital so that no more mice were produced. At left, the mouse is anesthetized. At right, surgery is performed.

critical terms

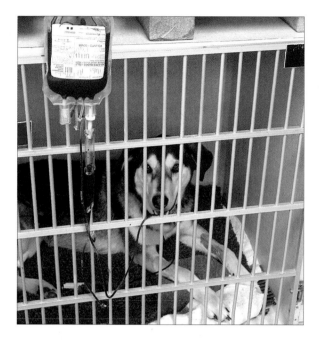

ABDOMEN: the belly area between the chest and the pelvis

ACTIVATED CHARCOAL: an antidote used to soak up poisons from the stomach and intestines

ACUTE ILLNESS: an illness that develops suddenly and severely

ACUPUNCTURE: the Chinese technique of inserting sterile needles at specific points in the body to treat pain and other medical conditions

ANOREXIA: loss of appetite in an animal

ANESTHESIA: loss of sensation or feeling. Doctors induce it with drugs during surgery to prevent animals from feeling pain.

ANESTHESIOLOGIST: a veterinary specialist who administers medicines that relieve pain in animals, especially during surgery

ARGUS INSTITUTE: an organization at the James L. Voss Veterinary Teaching Hospital that provides grief support for pet owners and trains veterinary teams to do the same

ARRHYTHMIA: an abnormal heart rhythm

BALL PYTHON: a snake that originates from West Africa and grows to be three to five feet long. They are called ball pythons because they curl into a ball when nervous or threatened.

BIOLOGY: the study of living organisms

BIOPSY: removal of tissue from an animal for examination under a microscope

BLOOD PRESSURE: a measurement of how well blood is moving through an animal's body

BLOAT: (see GDV)

CANINE: relating to dogs

CARDIOLOGIST: a veterinarian who treats heart-related problems in animals

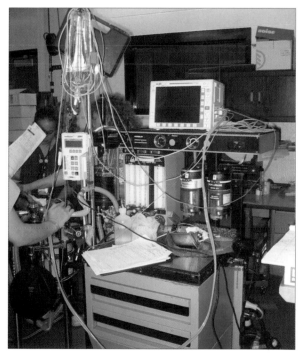

ABOVE, LEFT: This sweet-eyed dog receives a life-saving pint of blood donated by a fellow canine.

ABOVE, RIGHT: This anesthesia cart has all the equipment needed to anesthetize and monitor patients during surgery.

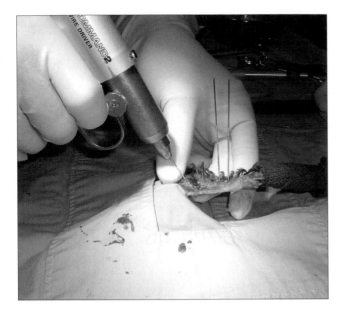

A vet repairs a bird's broken wing.

CATARACT: a cloudiness of the lens of the eye that reduces vision

CHRONIC ILLNESS: an illness that lasts for a long time, such as diabetes or asthma

COLOSTRUM: a fluid rich in antibodies that some animals produce just before and after giving birth. It's followed by milk production.

CPR: cardiopulmonary resuscitation

CRASH CART: a cabinet containing all the equipment necessary to treat an animal whose heart stops beating

CT (CAT) SCAN: a computerized x-ray that allows vets to view cross sections of an animal's body in detail

DEFIBRILLATOR: machine that sends an electrical shock through an animal's chest to jolt its heart back to a normal rhythm

DERMATOLOGIST: a veterinarian who diagnoses and treats animals' skin ailments, including allergies

DOMESTICATED ANIMALS: animals that are adapted to live in a human environment

ELECTROCARDIOGRAPH (ECG) MACHINE: an instrument that records the electrical signals from an animal's heart and charts them on a graph. It's used to identify and monitor heart problems.

ENDOSCOPY: a procedure that allows vets to look inside an animal's body using tiny cameras on tubes. It also enables them to take biopsies of tissue and remove foreign bodies without surgery.

ENDOTRACHEAL TUBE: a tube inserted into an animal's trachea (windpipe) to help it breathe

EQUINE: relating to horses

EXOTICS: a branch of veterinary medicine that treats animals such as birds, reptiles, and pocket pets (hamsters, rabbits, chinchillas)

FELINE: relating to cats

FOAL: a young horse

FOREIGN BODY: an abnormal object or substance in an animal's body

FRACTURE: a break in an animal's bone

GASTRIC DILATATION-VOLVULUS (GDV): a life-threatening condition in which a dog's stomach bloats (fills with air) and twists

INTERNAL MEDICINE SPECIALIST: a veterinarian who treats complex illnesses involving the body's organs and systems, such as the liver, pancreas, and immune system

INTRAVENOUS: entering the bloodstream through a vein

INTRAVENOUS (IV) FLUIDS: replacement body fluids given through a catheter (tube) placed in an animal's vein

MAGNETIC RESONANCE IMAGERS (MRIs): machines that create three-dimensional pictures of body organs using computers and magnetic energy (8,000 times more powerful than the earth's magnetic field)

MARE: an adult female horse

NEUROLOGIST: a veterinarian who diagnoses and treats nervous system disorders

ONCOLOGIST: a veterinarian who treats cancers in animals

OPHTHALMOLOGIST: a veterinarian who diagnoses and treats eye disorders

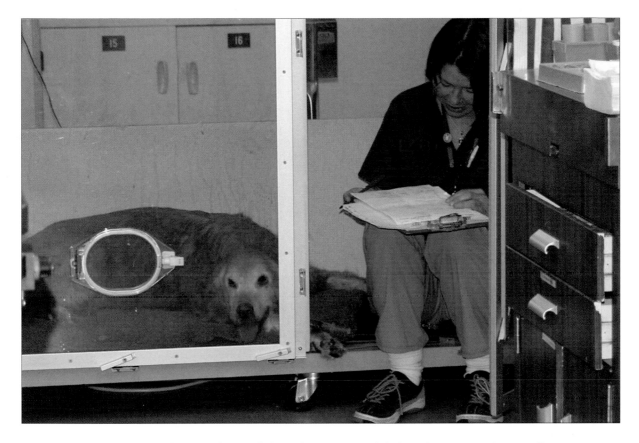

Veterinary technicians carefully monitor and chart the progress of their patients. Here, Sue Mordi reports on Barney's condition.

ORTHOPEDIC SURGEON: a veterinarian who repairs injuries to animals' bones and joints

PHARMACIST: a specialist who applies knowledge of drugs to animals and their unique characteristics and diseases

PNEUMOTHORAX: a collapsed lung caused by air trapped in the space between an animal's lungs and chest wall, which interferes with breathing

POSTOPERATIVE CARE: treatment after surgery

PACKED CELL VOLUME (PCV): the percentage of the blood that's made of red blood cells

PATHOLOGIST: a veterinarian who analyzes tissue, blood, and other samples to help diagnose diseases

RADIOLOGIST: a veterinarian who helps perform and assess x-rays, ultrasound, CT scans, and other ways of seeing inside the body

RESIDENT: a veterinarian seeking advanced training in a specialized area of medicine, such as emergency and critical care. Residencies generally run for three years.

RESPIRATION: the act of breathing

ROUNDS: meetings of doctors, veterinary students, interns, residents, and nurses to review and discuss cases

SOFT-TISSUE SURGEON: a veterinarian who removes foreign objects and tumors from animals

STETHOSCOPE: a tool vets use to amplify and listen to sounds made by the heart, lungs, and intestines

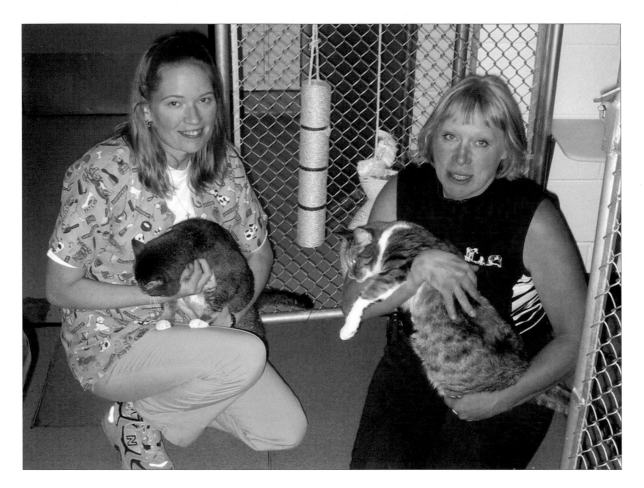

Colorado State University's Veterinary Teaching Hospital runs an animal blood donor program, coordinated by Kris Obssuth (left), and managed by Maura Green, head nurse for small-animal medicine. "The blood donor program impacts every area of the hospital," says Green, who along with Obssuth visits two blood donor cats.

TOXIC SUBSTANCE: anything that poisons or harms animals

TRIAGE: process by which an animal's medical condition is prioritized according to its severity

TUMOR: an abnormal mass of tissue that may or may not be cancerous

ULTRASOUND: an imaging tool that uses sound-wave technology to display an animal's internal organs

VETERINARIAN: a doctor who diagnoses and treats injuries, diseases, and disorders of animals

VETERINARY TECHNICIAN (NURSE): a person trained to assist a veterinarian with everything from medical and surgical procedures to anesthesiology and lab tests. Most states require that technicians pass an exam to become certified, licensed, or registered to practice.

VITAL SIGNS: the signs of life: heart rate, breathing, body temperature, and blood pressure

X-RAY (RADIOGRAPH): a diagnostic test that uses beams of electromagnetic energy to create images of animal bones and organs

ZOOLOGY: the branch of biology that studies animals and animal life

source Notes

EMERGENCY! Interviews with Dr. Tim Hackett and Dr. Vicki Campbell of Colorado State University's (CSU) James L. Voss Veterinary Teaching Hospital and ER observations.

ANIMAL ER Interviews with Dr. Tim Hackett, Dr. Vicki Campbell, Dr. Gary Stamp, Leslie Carter, MS, RVT, VTS; CSU's College of Veterinary Medicine and Biological Sciences, James L. Voss Veterinary Teaching Hospital Web site (www.csuvets.colostate.edu); American Animal Hospital Association (AAHA) Pet Owner Surveys 1999 and 2003; ER visits.

IS IT AN EMERGENCY? Interviews with Dr. Tim Hackett, Dr. Vicki Campbell; First Aid for Cats and Dogs course presented by the CSU Student Veterinary Emergency and Critical Care Society.

VETS AND PETS: A BRIEF HISTORY Interview with Dr. Susan Jones, author of *Valuing Animals: Veterinarians and Their Patients in Modern America*; Joanna Swabe, *Animals, Disease, and Human Society: Human-Animal Relations and the Rise of Veterinary Medicine* (London: Routledge, 1999), pp. 70–94; Anthony L. Podberscek, Elizabeth S. Paul, James A. Serpell, *Companion Animals and Us: Exploring the Relationships Between People and Pets* (Cambridge: Cambridge University Press, 2000) pp. 294–98; transcripts from *The Animal Attraction: Human Beings' Best Friends*, Australian Broadcasting Company, 2001 (www.abc.net.au/animals); 2003–4 survey of the American Pet Products Manufacturers Association.

HEALING HANDS Interviews with Dr. Tim Hackett, Dr. Vicki Campbell, Leslie Carter, Cheryl Spencer, Brenda Francis, Sue Mordi, Stephanie Pitzer, Amy Mahak—all of CSU's Vet Teaching Hospital; *A Career in Veterinary Technology*, brochure by the American Veterinary Medical Association (www.avma.com); ER visits.

LEARN THE LINGO Interviews with CSU's emergency and critical care team

SHELLEY: HBC Interviews with Brandy Perkins of Boulder County Animal Control, Dr. Jacob Head of the Animal Emergency Center in Longmont, Colorado, David and Jane Chaknova, Dr. Steve Benscheidt, Dr. Michael Walters, third-year emergency medicine resident at CSU's Veterinary Hospital, Dr. Erick Egger, small-animal orthopedic surgeon, CSU Veterinary Hospital, and anesthesia veterinary technician Kim Spelts; ER and family visits.

TOXIC TREATS Interview with Dr. Michael Walters; Charlotte Means, "The Wrath of Grapes," American Society for the Prevention of Cruelty to Animals (ASPCA) Web site (www.aspca.org), originally printed in the ASPCA's *Animal Watch* (Summer 2002) 22, no. 2.

LUCY SLIPS AWAY Interviews with Michelle Strong; Dr. Matthew Johnston, exotics medicine, CSU Veterinary Hospital; and Gail Bishop, coordinator, clinical services and community outreach, the Argus Institute for Families and Veterinary Medicine (www.argusinstitute.colostate.edu).

DEATH OF A PET Interviews with Gail Bishop and Bobbie Beach, clinical counselors at the Argus Institute for Families and Veterinary Medicine; *The Hardest Goodbye... Family Guide to Pet Loss*, booklet published by the Argus Institute.

RAISING CAIN Interviews with Nikki Cain and Gail Holmes of Double Dove Ranches in Longmont, Colorado, Dr. Judy Merriott, Dr. Darien Feary, Dr. Heather Connally, veterinary technicians Kim Ellis and Gina Gonzales, and vet student Mandy Chandler—all of CSU's Veterinary Teaching Hospital.

FIRST-AID KIT Interviews with the ER team and information gleaned from the First Aid for Cats and Dogs course presented by the CSU Student Veterinary Emergency and Critical Care Society.

Without blood donor animals such as these cats, many life-saving surgeries and other procedures could not be performed.

index

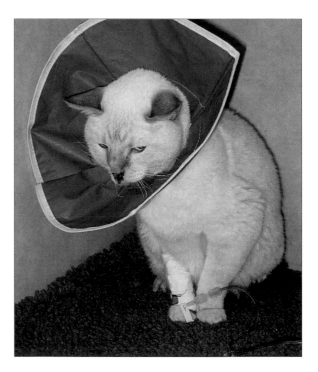

This cat is wearing an Elizabethan collar to prevent it from chewing on or biting the catheter.

Thanks for fixing me up!

Tucker, Paul,
& Cate Potgieter

To my friends in CCU thanks for taking such good care of me

- SPOOKY